FINAL BEGINNINGS

ALSO BY JOHN EDWARD

BOOKS

AFTER LIFE: Answers from the Other Side (with Natasha Stoynoff)
CROSSING OVER: The Stories Behind the Stories*
ONE LAST TIME: A Psychic Medium Speaks to Those We've Loved and Lost
WHAT IF GOD WERE THE SUN? (a novel)*

AUDIO PROGRAMS

CROSSING OVER: The Stories Behind the Stories (audio book)
DEVELOPING YOUR OWN PSYCHIC POWERS*
UNDERSTANDING YOUR ANGELS AND MEETING YOUR GUIDES*
UNLEASHING YOUR PSYCHIC POTENTIAL*
WHAT IF GOD WERE THE SUN? (audio book)*

*Also in Spanish

All of the above are available at your local bookstore,
or may be ordered by visiting any of the following
distributors for Princess books:
Hay House USA: **www.hayhouse.com**
Hay House Australia: **www.hayhouse.com.au**
Hay House UK: **www.hayhouse.co.uk**

FINAL
BEGINNINGS

John Edward
and Natasha Stoynoff

Princess Books
New York, NY

Published in the United States by: Princess Books, a Division of Get Psych'd, Inc., New York, NY

Distributed in the United States by: Hay House, Inc., P.O. Box 5100, Carlsbad, CA 92018-5100 • *Phone:* (760) 431-7695 or (800) 654-5126 • *Fax:* (760) 431-6948 or (800) 650-5115 • www.hayhouse.com • *Distributed in Australia by:* Hay House Australia Pty. Ltd., 18/36 Ralph St., Alexandria NSW 2015 • *Phone:* 612-9669-4299 • *Fax:* 612-9669-4144 • www.hayhouse.com.au • *Distributed in the United Kingdom by:* Hay House UK, Ltd. • Unit 62, Canalot Studios • 222 Kensal Rd., London W10 5BN • *Phone:* 44-20-8962-1230 • *Fax:* 44-20-8962-1239 • www.hayhouse.co.uk • *Distributed in the Republic of South Africa by:* Hay House SA (Pty), Ltd., P.O. Box 990, Witkoppen 2068 • *Phone/Fax:* 2711-7012233 • orders@psdprom.co.za • *Distributed in Canada by:* Raincoast • 9050 Shaughnessy St., Vancouver, B.C. V6P 6E5 • *Phone:* (604) 323-7100 • *Fax:* (604) 323-2600

Design: Summer McStravick

Library of Congress Cataloging-in-Publication Data

Edward, John (John J.)
  Final beginnings / John Edward and Natasha Stoynoff.
    p. cm.
  ISBN 1-932128-02-6 (hardcover)
  1. Manhattan (New York, N.Y.)—Fiction. 2. Supernatural—Fiction. 3. Spiritualism—Fiction. 4. Tunnels—Fiction. I. Stoynoff, Natasha. II. Title.

PS3555.D82F56 2004
813'.54—dc22

2004010725

ISBN 1-932128-02-6

07 06 05 04   4 3 2 1
1st printing, August 2004

Printed in the United States of America

With love to Vasilly Shamanduroff.

For Isobel, Jim . . . and Blake.

In the not-so-distant future . . .

CHAPTER 1

"THEY'RE CALLING IT 'THE CROWN OF GOD'—*la corona di Dio*," Giovanni said, dipping his oar into the dark water and delicately launching the gondola into the Venetian night.

La corona di Dio. Why does everything sound so much more romantic in Italian? Katherine Haywood mused, studying the shimmering turquoise light reflecting across the harbor. She followed the gondolier's gaze upward to the dazzling display of the aurora borealis illuminating the night sky with a circle of green fire.

Who comes all the way to Italy to see the northern lights? she wondered.

She knew why she'd come—for a desperately needed break, deliberately choosing a destination where she didn't speak the language, wouldn't be recognized, and where no one would stop her in the street asking her to connect them with a dead loved one.

As a psychic medium, easing people's pain over the loss of someone they'd loved had been her work and her life for nearly two decades. But after thousands of readings, Katherine was feeling tired, empty.

She wondered if she'd reached a point of "spiritual burnout." No matter how hard she worked, no matter how much heart she put into it, it never seemed to be enough.

If I could bring everyone's loved ones back from the dead so they'd be standing right in front of them, I would, Katherine thought. *But I'm just the messenger, not a miracle worker. And I'm one exhausted messenger.*

She listened to the soft waves of the lagoon lapping against the gondola, wishing the waters of the ancient city would wash her weariness away.

Katherine had never intended to be a famous psychic; she'd just wanted to use her abilities to help people. But like it or not, the fame had come, and the endless demands on her time and talents had quickly followed.

She hoped that putting an ocean between herself and her home would allow her to escape for a while, to tune out the world around her—and the world above. She needed to figure out how she'd reached this point: on the verge of abandoning what she considered to be her life's work, which she'd always believed was her destiny.

"They say these lights in the sky are being created by the biggest solar storm in nearly 200 years," Giovanni said, sliding his oar against the water. He spoke flawless English, but with a robust Italian accent.

She looked at the man sternly. She'd paid him $300 for the gondola ride—twice the going rate—on the condition that he didn't talk. She'd already read all about the unexpected space storm sweeping over the earth's atmosphere during her transatlantic flight. She didn't need a newscast from a gondolier; she just wanted to slip through the fabled city's watery roadways in peace.

"Some people are frightened by the sky. They say it's the end of the world. But others say it's a miracle, that the Blessed Mother is reaching out to—"

"Excuse me, Giovanni . . ."

"Hey, pretty lady, call me Johnny."

"Yes, all right . . . Johnny. I've just arrived in Italy today after a very long flight. I don't mean to be rude, but I did pay for a silent tour. So please . . . I just want a little quiet time right now to take in the sights. Okay? Thanks for understanding."

"Oh, sure, pretty lady. You don't want me to talk? I won't talk. I shut up like you ask."

In a flash, Katherine could see that the spirit world had no intention of letting her hide out. For a moment, the smiling gondolier wasn't wearing the traditional striped shirt and cap he'd been in when she climbed into the boat. The vision lasted only a second, but it was crystal clear: The man was wearing a Boston Bruins hockey jersey.

He'd approached her earlier on the pier with a grandiose "Ciao, bella donna." He assured her that he was a born-and-bred Venetian and would give the best water tour money could buy. But now she realized that his thick Italian accent and flirty-gondolier attitude were just typical tourist ploys.

She brushed the vision aside, hoping that her spirit guides weren't preparing to bring through all of the gondolier's undoubtedly chatty relatives who'd passed over to the Other Side.

They left the main lagoon, passing beneath a footbridge, and headed toward the heart of the old city.

"Hundreds of years ago, my ancestors named this bridge the Bridge of Sighs," Giovanni explained, "because condemned men sighed as they crossed it on their way to the prison tower." The word *tower* bounced off the tunnel walls and echoed in Katherine's ears like a tolling bell.

"Please, Giovanni . . . some quiet?"

"Oh, pretty lady, call me Johnny!"

"Yes . . . Johnny, now *please* . . ." Katherine said more insistently, "and if you're going to pretend to be a Venetian instead of a Bostonian, you could at least learn the local history. The bridge wasn't named by *your* ancestors, but by the English poet Lord Byron. And the condemned prisoners were led across the bridge to a *dungeon,* not a tower.

"I didn't say *tower* . . . I said *dungeon,*" Giovanni insisted, his Italian accent quickly dissolving. "I've given this tour a thousand times, and I've never said *tower.* And how the heck did you know I was from Boston? I've been doing this for ten years, and you're the first to ever guess."

"I never 'guess.'"

I was sure he said "tower," Katherine thought, as they glided silently though the ancient canals.

Katherine had hoped that this trip to Italy would recharge her emotional batteries, but already she was feeling worse than when she'd boarded the plane in New York.

I'm just jet-lagged. All I is need a good night's sleep, she decided, suddenly feeling claustrophobic.

As they moved quietly across the water, the walls of the buildings lining the canal seemed to be closing in on her. She tried to focus on the glowing night sky above, but her vision began to blur. A jumble of disconnected images burst through her mind: a handsome, dark-haired gentleman hugging a smiling little girl; a tired young man injecting himself with a strange-looking needle; a picnic basket; and the smoking barrel of a gun. A moment later, the gondola had pulled into the wide passage of the Grand Canal, and the images vanished.

Katherine shivered.

"Giovanni, I apologize—it's not you . . . I'm just suddenly feeling ill. Could you please take me back to the pier? I want to go to my hotel."

"No problem, pretty lady. But I think I've upset you. I'm sorry. Let me make it up to you . . . I'm taking a nice long drive through Tuscany tomorrow and spending the night at our family villa. If you've got no plans, please join me as my guest."

"I don't think so."

"Don't worry," he laughed. "My wife will be with us. And she barely says a word to anyone, especially me . . . so you'll have a quiet ride through the beautiful Tuscan countryside—vineyards, olive groves, beautiful rolling hills. Sounds good, no?"

"Well . . ."

"Tell you what . . . we'll stop by your hotel tomorrow morning, and if you feel like coming along, then come. If you don't, then don't worry about it. Nothing ventured, nothing gained, right?"

Olive groves and vineyards, Katherine considered. *That does sound like the perfect escape.*

"What time?"

"We'll be in front of your hotel at 8 A.M. Where are you staying?"

"The Hotel Pisa."

"Ah, the leaning tower . . . nice place."

Tower, tower, tower . . . the word reverberated through Katherine's mind.

KATHERINE WOKE AT DAWN feeling groggy and irritable. She was on her way outside to get some fresh air when the hotel concierge handed her a fax.

Great, I'm getting faxed, and no one's even supposed to know where I am, she thought. She was about to crumple it up and toss it into the Grand Canal without reading it, but decided to stick it in her purse until she'd found an open café and a triple espresso to wake herself up.

As she walked the cobblestone streets lining the canal, a group of early-rising Italian workmen began whistling and shouting at her.

"Buon giorno, signora bella! Mama mia! Bello dai capelli rossi! You 'av a date with me tonight, please?"

Katherine stood out in any crowd—a well-put-together red-head standing just over six feet tall was hard to miss. She favored well-tailored business suits in public, but today she'd dressed down for her countryside sojourn—jeans and a T-shirt.

"Sorry gentlemen, I'm married," she lied, holding up the wedding band she was still wearing five years after her divorce to ward off unwanted suitors.

"That's, how you say, a pity. Such beauty should never belong to only one man alone," one of them called out, as Katherine slipped into a café.

After drinking her second cup of espresso, she began reading the fax. It was a request from Daniel Dinnick in New York City to be a guest on his radio station later in the week.

The invitation was for the top-rated program in the city, so despite its ridiculous name—*The Jungle Hour*—and its particularly odious host, Katherine had appeared on it several times. Since it was widely syndicated, it was a fast and easy way to reach as many people as she could.

The fax was the standard request form: *Please join us on our Friday-morning show. . . .*

But it was odd that Daniel Dinnick, whose father was one of the world's wealthiest men, would send her a personal invitation. Those things were usually handled by booking agents or interns, not billionaires.

And how in heaven's name did he know where to find me? Katherine wondered.

She folded the fax and was about to return it to her purse when she felt a prickly tingle at the back of her neck—a sure sign that she was about to get a message from the Other Side. A moment later, she had an image of herself sitting with her father—who'd been dead five years—in a hospital room. He was shrunken and frail, in pain, lying on a bed with tubes running in and out of his arms. She was holding his hand, kissing his cheek, whispering to him that it was okay to let go . . . that family was waiting for him. The image morphed into another—a young girl receiving a chemo treatment, calling out for her mother but getting no answer.

Then the images were gone. She was back in the café, staring at the water taxis speeding along the Grand Canal. Getting sudden, unexpected images she didn't understand was nothing new to her—their meaning would eventually become clear. The Other Side was trying to tell her something . . . maybe that she was needed somewhere to help someone pass . . . maybe a sick little girl needed her help. She didn't know yet, but sooner or later she would.

She looked at the fax in her hand. *No . . . I'm done with all that,* she told herself.

Media appearances had helped her get her message across, and had hopefully eased the suffering of thousands of grieving people. But what had fame given her in return? A broken marriage, an empty Manhattan apartment, and a loneliness only worsened by being unaccompanied in one of the world's most romantic cities.

She was watching a pair of young lovers leaning against the canal bridge, kissing passionately, and began to rip up the fax when her eyes fell upon a single phrase that made her freeze: *at our new location in the BioWorld Tower.*

Katherine shook her head, looking up at the cloudless Venetian sky.

Come on, what's with all these tower references? She paid for her coffee and headed back to the hotel.

Katherine strolled through the narrow streets, peering into the windows of the shops that were just opening, and savoring the sweet aroma of freshly baked biscotti. A group of Italian schoolchildren walked past, laughing and carefree. It reminded Katherine of her own youth, and the day she'd first realized she was different from other kids, that she straddled two worlds—the world her parents and friends lived in, and the other world, the place where people who had died . . . lived.

She'd been crossing a busy street on the way to school in her Queens neighborhood when she dropped one of her schoolbooks. A strong gust of wind had blown the book into the street, and she'd begun to chase after it when she heard: *Kathy, you forgot to look both ways!*

She turned around, and there was her grandmother, who'd passed away more than a year before. A moment later, her grandmother vanished.

Katherine shook her head, thinking that her imagination was playing tricks on her, and then turned to retrieve her book, which was being flattened by a speeding bus. She jumped back from the curb, realizing how close she'd come to being under that bus herself.

"Thanks, Grams," Katherine said out loud.

You're welcome, my little Kathy, she heard a voice say in her head. In her mind she saw a quick image of a pink rose, and was flooded with the feelings of love she and her grandmother had always shared.

As she grew older, Katherine's ability to receive information from the Other Side, as she began calling it, grew more pronounced. She often knew who was on the phone before anyone answered it, and her best friends knew that if they lost something—a ring, a notebook, or a stuffed animal—she could picture the item in her mind and know where it was.

But on the night of her 13th birthday, she realized both the power—and the burden—of her ability. She was blowing out the candles on her cake and looking at her best friend, Caitlin, smiling at her from across the table. Suddenly, the room grew dark and she heard tires screeching on pavement. There was a flash . . . and a quick, vivid image of Caitlin's mother smashing through a windshield, then lying dead at the side of the road.

The vision vanished as quickly as it had come. Everything was normal again. They were singing "Happy Birthday," and Caitlin was smiling, passing her a big piece of cake. *What do I do now?* Katherine wondered, staring sadly at her friend, who was happily spooning chocolate ice cream onto her plate. *Am I supposed to tell her?*

After the party, Katherine walked Caitlin home and did what she thought was right: She told her about the vision, begging Caitlin to warn her mom not to drive.

"Why do you have to tell me stuff like that?" Caitlin asked, obviously upset by Katherine's words. "I don't want to hear it."

A week later, the accident happened exactly as Katherine had envisioned.

When Caitlin eventually returned to school, she wouldn't talk to Katherine, refusing to even make eye contact with her. Then one day Caitlin cornered her in the girls' bathroom. "What are you, *a freak?!*" she screamed at her supposed best friend. "Why didn't you *stop* it?"

Katherine didn't know what to say—she didn't have an answer. She got sick to her stomach and ran home in tears, shutting herself in her room and lying on her bed for hours, staring at the ceiling and trying to make sense of it all.

"Something's seriously wrong with me, Dad," she told her father when he came to get her for dinner that night and found her crying. She told him what had happened, and how her visions were beginning to terrify her. "Why do I see things like that when no one else does?"

"Don't you worry," he told her, dabbing her eyes with the corner of her pillowcase. "There's nothing wrong with you. You're special. Maybe I never told you this, but my mother was special in the same way." He smiled. "I think it just takes time to know what you're supposed to *do* with your specialness."

WHEN KATHERINE GOT BACK to the hotel, Giovanni and his wife were waiting for her in their Austin Mini.

"This is Vanessa, my beautiful wife," Giovanni said, greeting Katherine.

"Oh my God . . . you're the psychic from TV!" Vanessa shouted in Katherine's face. She turned and punched Giovanni in the arm. "Why didn't you tell me it was Katherine Haywood, you idiot?"

Vanessa turned back to Katherine, saying, "I'm your biggest fan . . . maybe you could talk to my uncle Gino who—"

"Excuse my wife, miss," Giovanni said. "She usually never says anything to anybody. I promise she won't pester you on the trip. I didn't even know you were a celebrity."

"Oh, you must get that all the time. I'm so sorry," Vanessa said, pulling her fingers across her lips. "My mouth is zipped from now on."

"Climb in," Giovanni instructed. "We're taking you to one of the most beautiful old cities in Tuscany—San Gimignano. They call it *la citta delle belle torri*."

"What does that mean?" Katherine asked.

"The city of beautiful towers. It has more medieval towers than any city in Italy . . . 13 altogether."

The color drained from Katherine's face. She leaned on the

roof of the Mini to steady herself and had a sudden mental image of a car bursting into flames and dropping into a river.

That's the East River, Katherine realized, as her head began to pound.

"Are you all right?" Vanessa asked.

"Um . . . I'm fine," Katherine replied, as another image flashed in front of her. This time it was a little girl—she thought it might be her niece, lying on a field of grass with the New York City skyline in the background. The girl was struggling to breathe—an oxygen mask was strapped to her face. She turned and looked at Katherine, her eyes pleading for help.

Katherine felt like she was suffocating. She couldn't catch her breath.

Something's terribly wrong, she thought.

She stepped away from the car and took a few deep breaths.

"I appreciate your offer, Giovanni, I really do," she said, quickly, "but something has come up . . . a family emergency. I wonder if you would be kind enough to wait for me to get my bags from my room and then drive me to the airport? I've got to get back to New York City."

I've got to get back home.

CHAPTER 2

THE PLANE DROPPED HUNDREDS OF FEET IN A FEW SECONDS, sending food plates flying and flight attendants tumbling into the aisle.

"This is your captain speaking, folks. No need for alarm—we've just hit a patch of unexpected turbulence." The pilot's voice was calm and controlled, intended to soothe his jittery passengers, but Katherine picked up on the man's nervousness and fear.

"Um . . . the small problem we're having has to do with this solar storm you might have heard about, the one giving us those beautiful night skies," the captain continued. "It seems to be getting worse, and it's messing up a few of our instruments just the tiniest bit. Nothing to worry about, mind you, but we might be in for a slightly bumpier ride than usual. So stay in your seats with your belts fastened, and we should have you at JFK in just under three hours. Relax and enjoy the rest of the movie."

Before the plane had taken off, Katherine had tried to call home to make sure her niece was all right, but the solar storm had created havoc with the phone lines, and she never got through. Now, she looked at the little overhead movie screen. Bruce Willis was machine-gunning bad guys on top of a skyscraper somewhere.

Another tower, she thought, leaning her head against the cold windowpane, catching scattered glimpses of the blue Atlantic through a broken patchwork of clouds.

Towers, towers, towers.

Whatever the message was, it had gotten her attention.

Her mind drifted back to the day the tower image had first become significant in her life. She'd been 18, still inexperienced and uncertain about her psychic talents. She was driving to the mall to buy supplies for her first day at NYU coming up the following week. She rolled down the car window and was singing along with John Lennon as her favorite Beatles song wafted through the radio speakers: *Juuuliaaaa . . . Juuuliaaaa . . . I sing my song of love . . . to reach you. . . .*

Katherine sped up to beat a yellow traffic light, but it turned red before she got there. She slammed on the brakes, stopping in front of the local community center, where she saw a banner hanging over the front door advertising a psychic fair taking place that day. On impulse, she pulled into the center's parking lot and bought a ticket at the front door for a psychic reading, writing her name in bold strokes on the little slip of paper.

The first thing she saw when she walked into the large gymnasium was a long row of psychics—some working with tarot cards, others using numerology—sitting behind foldout bridge tables. The tarot readers were flipping cards like they were playing solitaire. Katherine was transfixed, watching the cards roll through the readers' fingers, landing on their tablecloths with a loud *snap!*

She'd wandered past a dozen or so card readers, the Beatles tune still echoing in her head: *Juuuuuuliaaaa . . . calls meeeee . . .* when her eyes landed on a sign taped to one of the bridge tables: Julia Asher, Psychic Medium.

Katherine stopped in front of the table, and John Lennon stopped singing in her head.

Okay, assuming there are signs in this world, this has got to be one, Katherine thought. She sat down in front of the woman and handed her the ticket.

The psychic didn't look anything like Katherine had expected—this was no cheap carnival fortune-teller. The woman sitting in front of her was elegant and professional, wearing a simple navy skirt and white blouse, her glossy black hair carefully gathered into a French twist. She had the kind of face that was beautiful without any makeup, and a smile that instantly put Katherine at ease.

The woman looked at Katherine's name scribbled on the slip of paper and grinned.

"Hello, Katherine, my name is Julia . . . and you are the one."

"I beg your pardon?" Katherine asked uncertainly.

"Every time I'm at one of these fairs, or doing a seminar or group reading, I feel that there's one special person I'm supposed to reach," she explained. "Today, *you* are that person. I can feel it. Now . . . can I hold your ring for a moment?"

Katherine slipped her silver thumb ring into Julia's palm.

"What I'm doing is called *psychometry*," the woman said, cupping the ring in her hands. "I'm receiving energy from your ring, and I'm getting that you have a strong psychic connection . . . but you know that already, don't you?"

"Well . . . I've been able to . . . see things," Katherine told her, unsure how much of herself to reveal.

"You have very highly evolved spirit guides—guides working for the higher good of humankind. I think you have an important mission. . . ."

Katherine shifted uncomfortably in her seat. She felt like she was being recruited into some sort of cult, but still . . . she was beginning to instinctively trust this woman.

"There are powerful forces around you, Katherine. You're going to have to deal with a lot of death in your life, but you must remember that even the darkest tunnel can open up onto the brightest of lights."

"What do you mean?" Katherine asked nervously.

"I mean that every ending is also a beginning . . . nothing is final . . . everything is eternal."

"Holy cow," Katherine muttered, stunned by the older woman's intensity.

Julia laughed, handing Katherine back her ring. "Am I

freaking you out? I don't usually get quite so heavy on a first reading. But kid, you've got some powerful guides around you."

"Really?"

"No doubt about it . . . and I can tell that this is going to be your life's work. You're a born psychic. In fact, I think you're going to be famous one day—TV, radio, books, the works."

"Are you joking with me?" Katherine asked.

"Nope, but that's all in the future. You've got lots of work to do between now and then, and it's time for you to start learning the tools of your trade. These are called tarot cards," Julia said, shuffling the exotic deck.

For more than half an hour, the psychic turned over card after card and spoke of Katherine's future. She mentioned marriage, divorce, travel—and again, fame and fortune. Then she stopped and looked at Katherine with a serious expression. "This is the most important part of the reading. It will reveal when your true mission in life will begin . . . and it's the reason we're both here today. I need you to ask a question out loud, a question you *really* want answered."

Katherine was silent.

"Cat got your tongue?" Julia smiled.

"It just seems so . . . important. I don't know what to ask."

"I'll ask for you then. Okay?"

"Okay."

Julia closed her eyes and said, "Please give me one symbol that will let Katherine know when her mission is about to unfold."

Julia turned over the final card, placing it in the center of the table. It was a picture of a tall building with flames shooting out of the windows.

"It's the Tower card," Julia told her.

"LADIES AND GENTLEMEN, we're now beginning our final approach to JFK. Please make sure your tray tables are locked in their upright positions and your seat is brought all the way forward. . . ."

Katherine pulled out of her daydream.

The Tower card, she remembered. Her stomach tightened with remorse as she wondered—for the thousandth time—if she'd already missed out on her mission in life by not somehow stopping the 9/11 tragedy.

She'd been on a plane herself that horrible morning six years ago when the Twin Towers were attacked. Even though she'd had premonitions that something catastrophic was going to happen in New York City, perhaps even involving a plane, the feelings were too vague for her to interpret or act upon.

She knew in her heart that there was nothing she could have done to prevent what had happened—the universe had its own plans that day that didn't involve her. But that didn't stop scores of skeptics and critics from jumping all over her for her "intuitive lapse."

"If you're so psychic, why didn't you see it coming? Why didn't you stop it?" they'd ask accusingly.

She answered them by saying that she was only shown what she was meant to see . . . that no one can see God's bigger plan.

"I need you to put your seat up, Miss," a flight attendant said to Katherine, interrupting her reverie.

She adjusted her seat, looked down at the Manhattan skyline, and smiled, still basking in the memory of her first meeting with Julia—who would later become her mentor and a dear friend for many years.

As well as being a psychic, Julia was also a part-time poetry professor at NYU. They often got together after class to talk about books, philosophy, and, of course, all things psychic.

There had also been the many fun weekends when Julia invited her entire poetry class to visit her Hamptons beach house. Usually it was just the girls who'd show up. They'd get tipsy on wine, and laugh and sing, while Julia tried to get them to listen to her favorite Frank Sinatra tunes on a beat-up old record player.

"Don't you listen to any music from *this* century?" the girls would tease her.

"Hey, don't knock Frankie," Julia would say. "He's seen me through a lot of tough times. And 'Summer Wind' is one of the greatest songs ever written."

Over the years, in her relaxed, no-pressure way, Julia slowly built up Katherine's confidence in her own psychic abilities, and set her on a career path as a professional psychic.

Katherine built a solid reputation as an honest, highly gifted medium. She was so good that celebrity soon followed, along with all its complications. She was often too busy working to dedicate time to anything else. After a few strained years of marriage, her husband left her, complaining that she spent more time connecting strangers with dead people than she did connecting with him.

Soon after her divorce, Katherine lost Julia as well. Despite their closeness, her friend had never told her that she was dying of cancer until the very end. Julia's passing left a hole in Katherine's heart that had never quite healed.

Katherine had tried repeatedly to connect with her mentor on the Other Side, but had never succeeded. She couldn't understand why—she'd helped so many others reach lost loved ones, yet she couldn't do it for herself.

The tires of the 747 bounced off the runway. As soon as she had disembarked and was inside the terminal, Katherine called her sister to see if all was well with her niece.

"No problem here," her sister told her.

Then what the hell am I doing back in New York? Katherine wondered.

ON THE RIDE HOME, the radio in the taxi was tuned to WARP, the station owned by the Dinnick family, which aired *The Jungle Hour* every morning.

There's no way I'm going to do that show! Katherine thought.

But no sooner had the thought passed through her mind than she heard the nighttime DJ announce: "Make sure you tune in tomorrow morning. In our brand-new studio in the Dinnick BioWorld Tower, you'll hear the psychic of the century,

Katherine Haywood, taking calls on *The Jungle Hour,* with your host, Tarzan."

Katherine couldn't believe what she was hearing.

I'll be taking calls? I don't think so . . . I didn't even accept their offer to come on the show! She immediately called her publicist to chew her out.

"Kathy? I'm so sorry, but we had an intern in the office that day, and she must have given out your contact information. I tried to reach you, but the phones were all out." Katherine's publicist apologized profusely.

Katherine hung up and looked out the taxi window. A bus pulled up beside them with a huge billboard on its side, advertising Tower Records.

The tower again, she thought. *That must be why I'm here. Looks like I'll be at BioWorld Tower tomorrow doing their radio show after all. As Julia always said, every show or reading has a purpose . . . someone out there must need my help.*

EARLY THE NEXT MORNING, Katherine was greeted by a young woman as she entered the BioWorld Tower. The building was a post-9/11 phenomenon, hermetically sealed to protect against any kind of poisoned-air attack, with a security desk equipped with a metal detector, x-ray machine, and a device that took a personal DNA sample before allowing anyone to enter.

"Hi, Katherine, I'm Bronwyn, the show's production assistant. Don't worry about any of this crazy security business—it's *so* James Bond, just ridiculous . . . but I guess it's the times we live in, huh? I made sure you got celebrity clearance, so we can skip right through it," Bronwyn said, leading Katherine straight to the studio.

"I've got a confession . . . it could cost me my job, but I've got to tell you," Bronwyn continued. "It was me who faxed you in Italy. I even signed the boss's name to it. I couldn't help it— I dreamed every night for a week that I had to book you on the show today . . . it was the weirdest thing. But I just had to do it . . . so there it is. I don't care if you get me fired, but I always follow my intuition, no matter what. But I'm really, really sorry I wrecked your vacation." Bronwyn guided Katherine into the studio before the psychic had a chance to respond.

A minute later, she'd been fitted with a set of headphones and was sitting across from Tarzan, a tiny bald man with a booming voice, who had somehow become New York City's most popular disc jockey.

"AhhhhEEEEeeee AhhhhEEEEeeeee Ahhhhhhhh!"

Tarzan bellowed his obnoxious trademark, a poor Johnny Weissmuller imitation, into the microphone and through the headphones. Katherine's head began to pound, and she had an instant headache.

Tarzan put his hand over the microphone and whispered apologetically, "Sorry about that, Katherine. You know how New Yorkers love their wacky DJs."

His hand came off the mike and he was right back into character, letting out a few grunting ape sounds before introducing the morning lineup. Katherine thought he sounded ridiculous, but the Tarzan shtick worked very well for him. His morning show, for reasons Katherine couldn't fathom, had remained at number one in the biggest radio market in the country for years.

"AhhhhEEEEeeee AhhhhEEEEeeeee Ahhhhhhhh!"

Katherine cradled her head in her hands as Tarzan's yodeling cry blasted through her headset.

"Good morning, New York! I'm Tarzan, and we have a treat today for all you jungle animals out there. With me in the tree house is Katherine Haywood, one of the most renowned psychics in the world. She'll be taking calls in just a few minutes, but first a quick update on this weird solar storm that's been giving us the spectacular northern lights the last couple nights.

"Seems that no one was expecting this, and it's playing havoc with communications around the planet . . . get this, some scientists claim that if this storm intensifies, it will top the one way back in September 1859—the worst on record. That one actually *melted* telegraph wires, and set buildings on fire around the world . . . so expect some real communication problems today, folks . . . but hopefully that won't affect our first guest, the lovely Katherine Haywood, from communicating with the Other Side. . . . Good morning, Katherine, good to have you back on the show."

"Thank you, it's good to be here."

"I understand you just came back from a vacation in Italy. Sounds like fun."

"Um . . . it was a very short trip."

"Well, I'm really glad you're here with us, and I see the call board is lit up like a Christmas tree, so why don't we go right to the phones. Caller one, you're on the air with Katherine Haywood."

"Hi, Katherine, this is Evelyn."

"What can Katherine help you with today?" Tarzan asked. "Money? Work? Love life?"

Katherine began speaking before Evelyn had a chance to respond.

"I'm seeing a man on the Other Side with beautiful blue eyes. . . . I'm feeling a blackness in the pancreas and head. . . . He passed young, maybe early or mid-40s. I feel as if he wants me to tell you he sees what's happening in your life. . . . I think he's trying to tell me about your engagement or possibly a wedding."

There was the sound of gentle sobbing on the other end of the line.

"He's telling me he has Camille with him," Katherine continued. "They will both be at this event . . . I think it's your dad coming through. Does this make sense to you?"

"Oh, yes, absolutely. My dad passed away when he was 44 from stomach and brain cancer . . . and my mom, Camille, passed from a heart attack two months ago . . . and I'm getting married next month!" Evelyn cried into the phone. "Thank you, thank you so much, Katherine."

"Wow . . . right on the money," Tarzan said. "Let's go straight to another caller. Caller number two, what's your name, and what can Katherine help you with today?"

"Hi, Katherine . . . my name is Farah, and I just want you to know I'm such a big fan, and have friends who lost husbands who were New York firefighters when . . . well, you know. They were at one of your seminars, and you were so helpful to them."

"Thank you, that's special work for me, and very kind of you to say. Are you calling with a question about a K-N name . . . Karen, maybe?"

"Yes, exactly. My sister, she—"

"Don't tell me anything. I feel a head trauma . . . but also some fluid in the lungs . . . like she passed by drowning."

"Yes, yes," Farah said. "We found her in the lake near our cabin."

"Was there some police involvement with this . . . like a criminal investigation?"

"Yes, there was an inquest. She was such a strong swimmer that we thought—"

"Maybe she was murdered or committed suicide?"

"Yes, Katherine, that's what has haunted us."

"I'm seeing a cliff and water, and . . . my sense is that she was walking or hiking and slipped. She's showing me that she fell into the water and lost consciousness and drowned."

"That's what the coroner said, but hearing it from you means so much more . . . thank you."

"Wait . . . your sister is showing me pink roses, which means she's sending you her love . . . but I'm also getting . . . ."

Katherine's mind flashed with lightning-quick images of car wrecks and washed-out bridges.

"I think she's suggesting that you shouldn't drive today. Were you going somewhere in your car?"

"Just over the Queensboro Bridge into Manhattan to—"

"Whoa," Katherine interjected. "I'm not telling you what to do, but I'm getting a pretty strong sense you may want to get your car checked out or take the subway today."

"Okay, thanks again," Farah said.

"All right," Tarzan broke in. "Caller number three, you're on the air."

"Hi, Katherine, my name is Bob. This might sound silly compared to your other callers, but my dog is really old, and I'm wondering if when pets die—"

"Sorry to interrupt, Bob . . . but . . . are you calling from your car?"

"Yeah, I am . . ."

Katherine kept getting images of car wrecks . . . and then a collapsing tunnel.

"Are you in a tunnel?"

"No, but I was just heading to the Lincoln Tunnel . . ."

"I really don't have a clear fix on who's sending this, but my sense is that someone is telling me you should maybe avoid the tunnel today. If there's an alternate route, maybe you should consider it. . . ."

"Okay, I will . . . but, my question—"

"Is your dog's name Jay or Joe or—"

"Yes, Joe."

"Well, I hear him barking. There are pets on the Other Side, too. So if you're worried you won't be seeing him again, stop worrying. But really, reconsider the tunnel."

"Will do. Thanks again, Katherine."

"Seems like you're getting a lot of traffic reports from the Other Side today, Katherine. Are we seeing a psychic pattern here?" Tarzan asked.

"I'm not sure what that's all about," Katherine said, rubbing her temple, her head still throbbing. "I keep getting these images of . . . well, images of traffic mishaps, let's say."

"Interesting," Tarzan said. "All you animals driving out there better pay extra attention to the road. So, Katherine, let's not stick to local traffic, as we've got listeners out there from coast to coast. Do you have any predictions for next year's Oscars?"

"No, I'm not really picking up on celebrity news today . . . but I'm getting a lot of images of car wrecks, fire—there's a bridge burning somewhere. . . ."

"Really? Some kind of disaster . . . any idea where?"

"I just . . . I'm seeing the Oklahoma City bombing . . . and

I'm getting the month of September . . . I don't understand this . . . and they're showing me a helicopter crash . . . and a pair of handcuffs . . . it's all jumbled right now, and . . . I . . . I just don't know yet."

"Okay, well, let's go to our next caller . . . a man from Brooklyn. What's your name, sir, and what can Katherine help you with?"

"Help me? She can't help me at all. I just called to say I think it's disgusting that she pretends—"

"Now hold on, sir, no need to be rude. Miss Haywood has an impeccable—"

Katherine bolted upright in her seat and interrupted, "Caller, do you wear a uniform?" She tried to focus on an image in front of her.

"What did you say?"

"Do you wear a uniform?"

"You know damn well I do. I told your switchboard operator I was—"

"They're showing me that you wear a uniform—or you used to. I've got someone coming through loud and clear from the Other Side for you. I see a fire engine and a medal . . . a uniform and a gun. Is this making sense to you?"

"Listen, lady, what are you trying to pull? You already know I work for the—"

"Hold on . . . are you going on a red ski lift? Or something like . . . a cave? I see a dark cave. I'm at a loss here . . . do these things mean anything to you?"

"I don't ski, and the only cave I know about is the one you must have crawled out of . . . I called to say that I think your making a living on people's grief is the lowest—"

"I see fire all around you . . . there's smoke, I'm choking—"

"You should choke on your words, lady! You should be ashamed of yourself. Screw you and the broom you flew in on!"

There was the sound of a dial tone.

"Wait . . . Susan is coming through . . . she says it's not your fault . . . leave the gun alone . . . caller? Caller? Are you there?"

Tarzan was silently waving at Katherine to forget the caller. "Why don't we move on—"

"No. That man needs help. Can you trace that call? Get him back on the line!"

"Well, we can't really do that, and we're about to go to a commercial."

"No, don't, please . . . you have to get the man in the uniform back on the line. I need to tell him that Susan . . ." Katherine began coughing. Her head pounded.

"There's smoke . . . so much smoke," she continued. And then she blurted out a warning she couldn't believe she was making on a live broadcast, but it was out of her mouth before she could stop herself.

"Oh my God . . . oh my God! It's an explosion . . . many explosions . . . God, no . . . it looks like another attack. The explosions are going to happen here, in New York. Oh my God, it's going to happen today!"

Someone threw a switch in the control room, and the studio went silent. For a brief moment, there was nothing being broadcast on millions of radios across the country.

Nothing but dead air.

CHAPTER 3

JACK MORGAN OPENED HIS EYES AND WINCED. The familiar searing pain clawed into his hip and sliced toward his shoulder along the length of his spine—the same way it did every morning.

He'd been dreaming of Susan. He could still smell the lilac-scented French soap she loved so much. But now he was here, awake and alone. Gathering his strength, he rolled off the couch and got to his feet. A barely audible moan escaped through his lips.

Enough. Stop complaining, Jack thought, biting the inside of his cheek until he tasted blood.

He hated mornings most—the first minutes of consciousness before he got a grip on his near-constant physical pain and chronic loneliness. Mornings made him feel weak, and he hated weakness.

He pulled the bedding off the couch and stowed it inside the wicker chest, which doubled as a linen closet. He'd been sleeping in the guest room since Susan had gone. He couldn't bear to be in their bedroom, not even for one minute.

He spent an hour forcing himself to do 100 sit-ups and 200 push-ups. It was agony, but it was his routine, and routine was all that kept him going. He put on his uniform—jeans and a white, neatly pressed dress shirt and Army boots—then limped to the small bathroom in the corner to clean up. Few people ever saw him at all these days, but when he was on the job, he made sure he looked presentable and professional.

He was still a cop, and he wanted to feel like one.

Although he was in his 50s, Jack still had a full head of wavy black hair, and even though he cut it himself, it was always neat and regulation short. Now, he washed his face without looking in the mirror—he'd stopped looking long ago, not noticing the deep creases that years of pain had embedded in his face. But the creases hadn't destroyed the naturally boyish expression he'd always worn—and hated—his entire life.

Susan had never tired of kidding him about it. "Stop trying to hide it, sweetie," she'd say, whenever he tried to grow a mustache. "You'll always look like an adorable ten-year-old. What woman wouldn't want to love you to pieces?"

Jack toweled himself off and turned to face the day.

The morning sunlight flooded the guest room. The drapes were usually pulled tight throughout the house all day, but he must have left them open yesterday when he'd cleaned up—he'd washed the place from top to bottom so it would be spotless when he was found.

He was drawing the curtains when he spotted Mrs. Tirella—Mrs. T.—pushing her wire buggy of newspapers down the street. She was 72, but insisted on being called "the paper boy." She walked with the easy gait and reckless speed of a teenager. Her long gray hair was forever tucked beneath an ancient Brooklyn Dodgers ball cap.

Mrs. T. was one of a handful of local small-time criminals Jack had befriended in his Brooklyn neighborhood known as Park Slope. He knew that Mrs. T. spent no more than a dollar's worth of quarters at the newspaper boxes each morning, but she always managed to fill her buggy to the brim with fresh newsprint. Jack didn't mind, and had turned a blind eye to her petty larceny when he'd been walking the beat in Park Slope because he knew Mrs. T. had been dealt a tough hand. She'd been widowed just a few weeks after arriving in the country when her husband had come into some bad luck while walking home after his graveyard shift as night watchman at the Brooklyn Navy Yard. He'd survived just long enough to tell the tale.

One Christmas, Jack and Susan had Mrs. T. over for turkey dinner. Mrs. T. always brought her own homemade wine because Jack didn't keep any booze in the house. After she'd had a few glasses too many, Mrs. T. told them about her husband's brush with God.

According to her, Vito Tirella was just two blocks from their apartment on 7th Avenue when a DC-8 exploded in a massive fireball so close to him that his eyebrows were singed and the plastic tips of his shoelaces melted.

"He come in the door and told me he seen the souls of dead peoples leaving their bodies and floatin' up to heaven," Mrs. T. had confided to Jack and Susan in a conspiratorial whisper, crossing herself with her right hand and polishing off a tumbler of vino with her left.

"That's why God take him from me. Vito seen too much. After he told me the story . . . he kiss me, kiss the babies, and then—Santa Maria—he drop dead on the floor at my feet. But Capitano Jack, I swear . . . Vito, he still come to me every day to give me strength to go on."

Jack just nodded when Mrs. T. had spun him the yarn about her dead husband, and then he'd taken away her wineglass. He'd never been one for the hereafter. As far as he was concerned, once you were dead, you were dead—period, end of story. But the plane crash in Park Slope, well, that was not only fact, it was one of his most vivid childhood memories.

The jet had gone down on December 16, 1960—two days after his seventh birthday—just a few blocks from his house. It was a Friday morning, and he'd pretended to be sick so he could stay home from school and watch out for his mom, who'd "fallen down the stairs" and hurt herself pretty badly the night before after an argument with his drunken father.

He was lying on his bed watching big drops of freezing rain smack against his window like blobs of paste when the plane roared overhead and disappeared in a ball of fire.

He went up to his rooftop hideout and watched the fire-fighters carry dozens of body bags away from the site—but he didn't remember seeing any spirits flying around . . . at least he didn't think he had. There was a moment when . . .

Nah . . . , he thought, *that was just a kid's overactive imagination.*

The only one he saw giving up the ghost that day was his mother—she'd fallen down the stairs once too often. Jack figured that the plane crash had made her realize how fragile life was and that she wasn't going to waste hers being brutalized by an alcoholic husband.

He'd watched her from the roof as she walked through the burning neighborhood with a suitcase in her hand. But that was a long time ago, and Jack didn't like to think about it.

Mrs. T. tended to tell a few tall tales when she was on the vino, but she was a good woman who'd raised two boys on her own. And when Susan was out shopping or visiting her mother in the nursing home, she always had the old lady watch over their son, Liam.

Jack watched Mrs. T. make a sale to a couple of early-morning yuppies across the street lounging on the patio of Mimo's Authentic Neapolitan Bistro. He remembered when Mimo's was called Mo's Deli, after its owner, Mohammed Shahmah. Mohammed had discovered that a trendy name change was a perfectly legal way to sell a nickel's worth of coffee and a few drops of steamed milk for $3.50.

This used to be such a nice, affordable family neighborhood, Jack thought, looking at the yuppies whose kind had all but taken over Park Slope.

"*Buon giorno,* Capitano Jack . . . you like I should bring you up a free paper?" Mrs. T. had spotted Jack standing in the second-story window and started waving *The Trumpet,* one of New York's notoriously trashy tabloids, at him.

Jack shook his head silently at the old woman. He hadn't spoken to her or anyone else in the neighborhood for years—he wasn't going to start entertaining visitors now, not today of all days.

"You no take a paper since they put you picture on the front page when Mrs. Susan was . . ."

Mrs. Tirella chopped her sentence so hard Jack heard her dentures clack from the street.

"I'm so sorry, Capitano . . . I got big mouth. I talk too much. Please, I'm so sorry," Mrs. Tirella kept apologizing, but Jack had drawn the drapes.

He limped from the guest room to the long hallway, where the few memories he allowed himself were neatly arranged on the wall in a single row of framed photographs.

He called it "the family gallery." Fifteen photos in all, one for each year of his marriage. There wasn't a single photo from his childhood: no snapshots of his parents, summer holidays, or smiling grandparents. As far as Jack was concerned, his life began when he met his wife.

"We weren't what you'd call a 'Kodak moment' kind of family," Jack had told Susan when asked about the lack of memorabilia. "You've heard of a mean drunk? My old man was mean sober and a murderous bastard after a few drinks. He beat on my mom until she left, then he beat on me until I could beat him back. And that's about all I've got to say about my family."

What amazed Jack was that, despite his contempt for his father, he'd ended up just like him. He'd become a cop and a bitter, mean drunk—until he met Susan and gave up the booze for good.

Jack continued down the hall as he did every morning, pausing before each picture until his legs began to ache so much that he had to move along.

He lifted the first photo off the hook and held it in both hands. The image was of him and Susan huddling together in front of Niagara Falls on their honeymoon. They were wearing rain slickers and we've-just-won-the-lottery smiles. Jack was holding Susan's left wrist toward the camera, and Susan was hamming it up, displaying her ring finger with a dramatic flourish, as though the diamond weighed a pound. But Jack had been so broke when he bought the ring that he'd needed the jeweler's magnifying glass to see what he was getting for a week's pay. It was just a tiny chip of a rock, but in the photo it had caught the rainbow reflection from the falls and was sparkling like a star. Later he tried to buy a bigger diamond, but Susan didn't want one. That was her way.

"Why tamper with perfection," she'd said.

Jack had never figured out what she'd seen in him. The first time they met, Jack was lying facedown, drunk and unconscious on the street outside a Flatbush Avenue dive bar. Susan took pity on him and practically carried him to her apartment, where she let him sleep it off on her couch. The next morning she plopped a hot mug of coffee in front of him and said that he shouldn't treat himself so poorly because "tomorrow will be a better day."

It was the first thing she ever said to him, and she'd repeat it whenever the job or money troubles got him down. She must have said it a million times, and he never tired of it. *Tomorrow will be a better day.*

They were married 12 months later, on the first anniversary of Jack's sobriety.

Jack returned the honeymoon picture to its place and continued down the hall.

The next photo was of Susan, her wedding dress hiked up to her knees and her wild perm of dark hair poking out from the bottom of her American flag motorcycle helmet. She was straddling the seat of Jack's Harley minutes after they'd taken their vows at City Hall. Susan had wanted a church wedding, but Jack refused. He didn't believe in God, and said if heaven and hell existed, they could be found in New York City, just below 14th Street.

The next picture was of the two of them laughing, holding buckets over their heads to catch the rain streaming through the ceiling of the Catskill Mountain cabin they'd rented each summer.

Then there was the picture of Susan in a hospital bed cradling two-hour-old Liam—the boy's pink face wrinkled up like an old man, and Susan grinning ear-to-ear despite enduring 18 hours of labor.

Beside that was the Polaroid of Liam at age nine—his mop of auburn hair exploding in all directions, wearing the flannel cowboy-and-Indian pajamas he'd loved so much. He was posing in front of the Christmas tree they'd chopped down themselves in Connecticut, proudly displaying his new, four-foot-long fire engine with the "authentic" clanging brass bell and extendable ladder.

Jack remembered that Liam had begged him for the truck for nearly a year. The boy had wanted to be a fireman since he'd learned to talk. The last picture on the wall was of Liam in his new uniform just after he'd finished his training with the New York Fire Department.

Jack looked at the pictures but felt nothing.

In the first years after Susan had died, he'd let the images pull him back through time—past the pain to a place where he could briefly relive those happy moments. But he stopped doing that after Liam had left as well.

Now, he studied the images like crime-scene photos, focusing on details: Susan's earrings, Liam's Band-Aid—searching for something that might yield a hidden clue that could explain his ruined life.

At the end of the hall, Jack slid back the lid of his grandfather's rolltop desk and picked up a yellowing, ten-year-old tabloid newspaper with a banner headline that screamed from the past: TOP COP SHOT; WIFE RAPED, MURDERED.

Six words. A simple phrase that, like his marriage, had ended with *murder.* Under the headline, there were two photos vertically dividing the front page. On the left was Jack's NYPD graduation photo; on the right was Susan, but you wouldn't know it. She was just another nameless corpse on a New York street—a red circle soaking through the white sheet covering her body.

Jack didn't have to read the story; he could recite it as easily as rattling off Miranda rights:

The wife of a New York City police captain was raped and shot dead in Central Park last night as her husband of 15 years, Captain Jack Morgan, lay bleeding and helpless on the ground just three feet away.

Police spokesperson David Kelly said the Morgans were celebrating their 15th wedding anniversary with a carriage ride through the park when they encountered four youths attacking a female jogger.

According to police and witnesses, Captain Morgan jumped from the carriage and went to the jogger's defense. One of the youths pulled a handgun and shot the heroic cop three times: in the leg, hip and back, narrowly missing his spinal cord.

The men, described as white males in their late teens or early 20s, then pulled Mrs. Morgan from the carriage and sexually assaulted her before shooting her once through the heart. The suspects were last seen fleeing through the park toward Strawberry Fields.

"It was terrible what those punks done—they were so happy in the carriage, holding hands and kissing like a couple of kids," said hansom cab driver Nicholas Copland.

"I ran after the jogger to see if she was all right, and when I got back there was blood everywhere and the lady was dead."

Captain Morgan remains in Roosevelt hospital in critical condition. The attackers are still at large, but police say they have the name of at least one of the suspects.

Jack traced his finger over the image of Susan's corpse. He couldn't remember anything about that night. He had to piece it together from what he'd been told or what he'd read.

AT FIRST THE PAPERS called Jack a hero; the entire city seemed to empathize with his loss. But the sympathy didn't last. The papers had turned on him before he'd checked out of the hospital. It happened when a priest turned up at his bedside four weeks after the attack, assuring Jack that Susan was "in heaven with God." Even though he was in traction, Jack nearly killed the man, fracturing the priest's skull and breaking his jaw in two places.

The next day's headline read: CRAZY JACK SMACKS PRIEST. The article explained that Jack had been insane with grief when he'd attacked the priest, but the name Crazy Jack stuck. It hadn't helped that an unidentified nurse had been quoted as saying that Jack had spit on the priest while beating him about the head with a bedpan.

Then there was the trial 18 months later. The boys who killed Susan had been caught and convicted of second-degree murder, but Jack refused to go to the courthouse, even for the sentencing. When a reporter showed up at his house to find out why, Jack said, "Because they're not guilty; they didn't kill her."

It was the last time Jack had ever talked to anyone about Susan's murder, and the last time he landed on a tabloid's front page.

CRAZY JACK CLAIMS COPS GOT IT WRONG; WIFE'S KILLERS INNOCENT!

Jack didn't care. As far as he was concerned, the story was true. *He* was the one who'd taken Susan into the park that night and put her at risk by playing hero. It didn't matter how many lowlifes they locked up—in his mind, his wife's killer was still free. Jack Morgan murdered Susan; there was no doubt about it.

But that was nobody else's business. He hung up the phone when concerned relatives called, and closed the door on consoling neighbors. Jack wouldn't even talk about the murder with Liam, who, after he was grown, stopped by the house every weekend to check up on his dad. They talked about sports and Liam's career, but never about the murder. Then one weekend the visits stopped. Jack never saw his son again.

Due to his injuries, Jack was declared unfit for active duty, but he was years away from retirement. He offered to serve out his time working homicide cold cases from his home. The police chief was only too happy to oblige, and to get Crazy Jack out of the public eye.

His living room was soon crammed with stacks of cardboard boxes filled with files on long-forgotten murders. Jack phoned in his reports at first, but eventually taught himself to use a computer. Once he could communicate over the Internet, he basically never left his house.

That had started ten years ago. It would end at 5 P.M. today, when he would be officially retired from the NYPD.

JACK TOOK A LAST LOOK at the young face staring up at him from the old newspaper, then let the tabloid fall to the floor. On the desk in front of him sat three carefully arranged items: his service revolver and two silver medals.

The first medal arrived in the mail from the Fire Department of New York in the winter of 2001. He slipped it into the front pocket of his jeans without looking at it.

The other medallion was heavier, a commemorative reward from the NYPD for wounds suffered the night Susan was killed. He looked at the Latin words embossed on its face. *"Fidelis Ad Mortem . . .* faithful unto death," he whispered. "Well, I have been." He dropped the medal back on the desk, picked up his service revolver, and carefully walked downstairs.

Jack maneuvered around the neatly stacked corridor of cardboard case files lining his living room before reaching the kitchen and flicking on the radio. He put his gun on top of the counter, thinking of Susan's mantra: *Tomorrow will be a better day.*

Well, for the first time in ten years, tomorrow actually will *be a better day,* Jack thought.

He turned on the radio and began fiddling with the tuner. At first there was just static, then he hit a clear signal.

"AhhhhEEEEeeee AhhhhEEEEeeeee Ahhhhhhhh!"

What the hell is this? Jack wondered, quickly turning down the volume. He was about to tune in to another station when he heard the name of the upcoming guest: psychic Katherine Haywood.

There were three types of people Jack couldn't stomach: reporters, priests, and psychics. He remembered this particular psychic's name from several cold cases he'd worked on . . . the files all said that she'd actually helped find the bodies of the victims, even though the murderers hadn't been found. In all the cases, the officers involved had praised Katherine Haywood as a professional and said that she'd been extremely helpful— both during the investigation and in helping the victims' families cope in the aftermath.

Jack didn't buy it. He thought she had everybody fooled and was probably making a good living from people's suffering. For all he knew, she'd committed the crimes herself for the publicity.

He turned up the radio, grinding his teeth as he listened.

"He's telling me he has Camille with him. They will both be at this event . . . I think it's your dad coming through. Does this make sense to you?"

This is obscene, Jack fumed. *Listen to this grief hustler, leeching off that woman's pain.*

He turned up the radio even louder.

" . . . my mom, Camille, passed from a heart attack two months ago . . . and I'm getting married next month. Thank you, thank you so much, Katherine."

Jack picked up the phone, dialed 411, and got the number for WARP. His heart was pounding like a rookie patrolman making his first bust when the receptionist picked up the phone

"Good morning. WARP. How may I direct your call?" the woman asked.

"It's about this so-called psychic you have on the air. I'm a cop, and I know about the missing persons and homicide cases she worked on—"

"Where are you calling from, sir?"

"What? What difference—from Brooklyn, but—"

"Please hold."

"Hold? No. I won't hold. I just want you to know this woman is a phony and a liar, and you people should be ashamed for letting her . . . Hello? Hello?"

". . . a man from Brooklyn . . . what's your name, sir, and what can Katherine help you with?"

"Help me? She can't help me at all. I just called to say I think it's disgusting that she pretends—"

"Now hold on, sir, no need to be rude. Miss Haywood has an impeccable—"

Katherine interrupted, "Caller, do you wear a uniform?"

"What did you say?"

"Do you wear a uniform?"

"You know damn well I do. I told your switchboard operator I was—"

"They're showing me that you wear a uniform—or you used to. I've got someone coming through loud and clear from the Other Side for you. I see a fire engine and a medal . . . a uniform and a gun. Is this making sense to you?"

"Listen, lady, what are you trying to pull? You already know I work for the—"

"Hold on . . . are you going on a red ski lift? Or something like . . . a cave? I see a dark cave. I'm at a loss here . . . do these things mean anything to you?"

"I don't ski, and the only cave I know about is the one you must have crawled out of . . . I called to say that I think your making a living on people's grief is the lowest—"

"I see fire all around you . . . there's smoke, I'm choking—"

"You should choke on your words, lady! You should be ashamed of yourself. Screw you and the broom you flew in on!"

Jack slammed down the receiver.

Of course she'd say she saw a uniform, I told the receptionist I was a cop. Damn phony! I can't believe I let her use me like that.

Jack picked up his gun from the counter and moved as quickly as he could to the living room. He opened the six-cylinder on his .38 and dropped in the single bullet he'd been saving for a decade. He'd been planning to check out at 5 P.M. on the nose—the end of the workday and his career—but the psychic had him so riled up that he couldn't wait one more second to end it all.

He stepped onto the large plastic sheet he'd spread out on the floor after he'd cleaned the house, and planted the muzzle of the .38 into the soft tissue between his chin and Adam's apple. Closing his eyes, he tightened his finger on the trigger . . . then he heard Katherine's shrieking voice echoing from the kitchen.

"Oh my God . . . oh my God! It's an explosion . . . many explosions . . . God, no . . . it looks like another attack. The explosions are going to happen here, in New York. Oh my God, it's going to happen today!"

Jack froze. In an instant, all the emotions he'd repressed for years surged through his body.

"Now you've gone too far, lady!" he yelled in the direction of the kitchen. "You're feeding off the fears of a whole city!"

Jack stumbled to the hall closet, pulling out his leather jacket and helmet. He tucked his gun into his jacket.

"I'm going to put the fear of God into that fraudulent bitch!" he yelled, stepping out of his house with a true purpose for the first time in years.

CHAPTER 4

"WE GOT A FLOATER IN THE EAST RIVER. . . ."

Zoe Crane's fingers froze in mid-stroke, the plastic staccato clacking of her keyboard falling silent.

"Did you copy, Central?"

Zoe cocked an ear toward the police-scanner room on the other side of her cubicle. Her eyes darted to the travel clock by her computer, her hands hovering over the keyboard. She sucked her lower lip between her teeth.

Her *AstroChart* column was due in three hours, and she hadn't even gotten to the earth signs yet. The managing editor was looking for any excuse to crucify her; and handing in late copy would be like donating nails for the cross. But she couldn't help herself. She was a cop reporter through and through, and a hard-news junkie, addicted to the electronic chatter of the police scanner. Besides, a good floater was a guaranteed shot at the front page.

A serious reporter by trade, Zoe had been banished to do horoscopes and fluff pieces for the lifestyles section of the newspaper. She didn't buy any of this zodiac nonsense and usually let Carolyn, her assistant and a true astrology fanatic, write all the horoscopes. But Carolyn had called in sick today, leaving Zoe in a real jam.

"Say again, Harbor Unit 2 . . . was that a 'boater' on the East River?"

"Negative, Central . . . a floater . . . possible 1029. We're a couple hundred yards out, but through the binoculars it looks like a female, faceup in the water and definitely DOA. She's snagged on the rocks at the bottom of the bridge support."

"The Queensboro Bridge—is that affirmative, Harbor 2?"

"Affirmative, Central—Queensboro Bridge, at the support pillar on the Manhattan side of Roosevelt Island."

"Okay. 10-4, Harbor 2 . . . East River floater under the Queensboro Bridge, west side of Roosevelt Island. Check it out and report back."

"10-4, Central . . . but . . . uh . . . we're stationed here as lead security detail for the mayor and governor's arrival . . . Harbor 2, over."

"Copy that, Harbor 2 . . . stand by for instructions."

Under the Queensboro Bridge? That's practically right beneath our office . . . I bet I could see it from the scanner room, Zoe considered.

Her fingers dropped to the keys, her eyes focusing on the planetary-chart cheat sheet Carolyn had taped to the edge of her computer screen. She took a deep breath, exhaled slowly, and began typing.

Sagittarius: You've been too self-indulgent for too long! Dwelling on your problems while ignoring the needs of others has left you spiritually bereft and emotionally stunted. Nourish your soul by doing a good deed or selfless act for someone else—and do it soon! Work also looms large this week—time to think of a career change?

Zoe stopped typing, and started to laugh. *I can't believe how accurate these things can actually be. I'm a Sagittarius, and this prediction is dead on. I really do need a career change, and it doesn't look like I'm going to get it here.*

But if she wanted to keep working at *The New York Daily Trumpet,* she had to bite the bullet and put her name on this fluff, at least until she could get her hands on a *real* news story again. And that wasn't going to happen until either the managing editor dropped dead from a heart attack or some Pulitzer Prize–winning story landed in her lap.

What galled her the most was that she didn't believe a single word of the psychic mumbo jumbo she had to write about.

Zoe stood and stretched, her calf muscles cramping from the workout her boxing trainer had put them through that morning. She actually liked the pain; it meant she was getting stronger, and she hated the thought of ever being at a disadvantage. Besides, the boxing kept her mind sharp, and she needed that, especially this week.

She checked her work calendar, groaning at the heavy load. There were weekly horoscopes due by noon, a feature on the Manhattan Ghost Finders' Club due by 6 P.M., and a palm-reading class to attend so she could write a scathing article on those phony psychics who were all over Manhattan. Then there was that stack of mail from her "fans" that she had to respond to.

Zoe picked up the first letter from a large stack of envelopes on her desk, and her stomach knotted slightly. The letter had obviously been written by a child. It had no return address, there was a picture of a pony drawn on the envelope in crayon, and it was covered with little paste-on stars. She read the badly misspelled letter:

Dear Zoe,

I love your collimns about horriscopes and read them everyday. I live in a foster home now, but I use to live on a farm and had a pony like this one. If I move to anuther farm, I will get another pony and name it Lucky Stars, like after your collimn.

Your big fan,
Cassandra

Zoe stared at the letter for several minutes. "Cassandra" was Zoe's favorite name. She even used it as the password to log on to her computer.

If I ever have a daughter, if I'd only been able to . . . stop it!
That's enough sentiment—the past is the past, she reminded herself, tucking the letter back into the envelope and tossing it
into the trash.

A moment later, she pulled it out.

Well, it is kind of sweet, she thought, and pinned it to her bul-
letin board, next to the picture of her dog, Rewrite, a little border collie she'd had since moving to New York. She'd found him
on the street near Columbia University, shivering and half-
starved.

"You're a stray just like me," Zoe said, when she took him
back to her room. Rewrite was the only thing she'd ever
really loved since leaving New Jersey. But he'd gotten old and
sick with cancer, and she had to have him put him down just
last week.

Don't think about that . . . back to work, what else do I have to
do? Oh yeah, I can't forget the ultimate bullshit artist herself! She
remembered that in five minutes, celebrity psychic Katherine
Haywood would be on the radio.

Exposing the country's best-known and most-respected psychic as
a fraud could be a one-way ticket back to serious reporting.

Zoe had already caught a few fraudulent psychics red-
handed since being stuck on this beat, but they were your typical fortune-teller types or those 1-900-dial-a-psychics.

No matter how hard she studied Katherine Haywood's style
on the radio, on TV, or at seminars, Zoe had never been able to
discover how she did it. But she still wasn't about to believe any
of it—not until she saw some hard evidence. She was convinced that Katherine had a sophisticated con-artist system
going, and sooner or later she'd figure it out. She'd even implied
as much in one of her columns, but still didn't have the hard
facts she needed to put her out of business.

"Harbor 2 . . . you're cleared to check out your floater. Harbor 3 will cover your security detail. . . ."

"10-4, Central. Proceeding to the bridge pillar."

"And Harbor 2, don't take the body onto the island;

transport it to Manhattan by boat—we don't want to ruin the mayor's ribbon cutting at the new BioWorld Center by dragging a corpse in front of the TV cameras."

"Copy that. Will do, Central. We'll hide the stiff from hizzonner and the cameras. Harbor 2 out."

Zoe leaned back in her chair, past the edge of her cubicle, peering at the two night-shift reporters assigned to the scanner room. She called them Sleepy and Dopey, because no matter how loud the police scanners chattered, they kept dozing. Today was no exception: A floater in the river, and they were sleeping in their swivel chairs—two pasty-faced old-timers dreaming their way to retirement.

A floater was a homicide or a suicide—and either could be a huge story. It's right outside their window and they don't even know it's happening. Zoe scowled, picking up her new palmtop computer with the super-zoom camera lens and strolling nonchalantly into the scanner room.

Through the window, Zoe could see that the Queensboro Bridge was busier than usual. She looked down at the East River and across to Roosevelt Island, where a crowd was gathering for the opening of Bioworld's new Supercomputer Re-Creation Center.

Zoe zoomed in on the crowd. There were plenty of cops, a bunch of balloons, what looked like a string quartet, and maybe a dozen or more members of the city council that she recognized. She focused in on the bridge's support pillar and followed it down to the water.

"Bingo . . . thar she blows," she whispered, bringing the NYPD police boat into the crosshairs of the lens. An officer was tossing a hook out toward the shore of the island. Zoe pressed the shutter button, and the camera beeped softly as she followed the rope to the corpse.

That looks weird, she thought, snapping a few more shots before the police scanner kicked to life again.

"Central, this is Harbor 2."

Sleepy and Dopey stirred in their chairs as Zoe slipped by

them and back to her cubicle.

"Go ahead, Harbor 2."

"Central, it's negative on the 1029. The floater is a Miss Bloomingdale. She's caught up in some old fishing cable or something. We'll be a while cutting her loose from the bridge piling."

"Okay, copy that, Harbor 2. Let us know when you're done. And boys, do be gentle with her. Central out."

So much for the front page, Zoe concluded. A "Miss Bloomingdale" meant a department-store mannequin.

But it might have been Jimmy Hoffa they found in the river, and those two guys would have slept through it! And these losers are my replacements?

Zoe had come a long way from Trenton, New Jersey. Until a year and a half ago, she'd been the top police reporter in New York City and had broken more crime stories than any other journalist in the city—probably the entire country. And she didn't have to slum around cop bars or sleep with desk sergeants to do it. She'd never once cashed in on her looks to get ahead— she'd left all that behind in Jersey.

She'd seen too many hard-luck cases in New York to whine about being born blonde and beautiful. But the truth was . . . good looks had always been her biggest handicap.

From the age of four, Zoe's adopted mother—the "evil step-mother," Zoe called her—had forced her into one beauty pageant after another. Zoe just wanted to ride her bike and play sports like other kids, but it wasn't to be.

"You got looks, and those looks pay the rent. So stop complainin'. Maybe you'll meet a nice guy," was all her mother would say about it.

Just before her 16th birthday, she did meet a nice guy, a local college boy. He proposed when she told him she was pregnant, and they planned to get married before the baby was born. But Zoe's mother put an end to that. She wanted her daughter to go all the way to Miss America.

"And you ain't gonna do that with a kid," she'd said.

Her mother threatened to have Zoe's boyfriend charged with statutory rape if he didn't disappear. Then she forced Zoe to give up the baby for adoption. Zoe wasn't allowed to see the newborn, and never even knew if she'd given birth to a boy or a girl.

Zoe barely spoke a word to her mother for the next two years.

As soon as she graduated from high school, she cut off her long blonde hair, took the money left over from her pageant winnings, got on a bus for New York City, and said good-bye to Trenton and her mother forever.

She studied journalism at Columbia University and then focused solely on her career. She swore off men forever, and the only release she allowed herself was two hours a day of boxing at a local gym. Her boxing coach, a wiry old Irishman who called himself Wildcat, had been a former featherweight champ. Now he was a part-time night watchman at the city morgue and would occasionally sneak Zoe in after hours so she could study forensic reports. She was determined to be the city's best crime reporter, and figured that learning what crime looked like up close was one of the best ways to get there.

Zoe landed her first real job as a gofer at *The New York Daily Trumpet,* the best-selling tabloid in New York City. She had loftier ambitions, but it was a good place to start. A few years later, she got her big break—covering a drive-by shooting in Spanish Harlem that left three young brothers lying dead in the doorway of their housing complex.

According to police, the kids were caught in the cross fire of rival drug dealers—wrong place, wrong time. Every news organization in the city was vying for an interview with the family, but the police had sealed the block off.

It was Zoe's day off, but she headed uptown anyway just to see what was going on. She was hanging back from the pack of reporters who were surrounding the victims' apartment when she spotted a pizza guy delivering to the neighbor next door.

"Fifty bucks for your pizza and hat," she said.

"This pizza is spoken for, lady, and the hat is property of Tony's Pizzeria—for official company use only," the pizza man said, brushing past Zoe.

"Make it a hundred," Zoe yelled to his back. The pizza man turned and said, "Well, when you put it that way, all I can is say is . . . sold!"

A few minutes later, Zoe was in official pizza-company uniform, standing beside the yellow crime-scene tape, nodding to the patrolman.

"For the family," she said, holding up the pizza box.

"Go ahead," the patrolman said, lifting the tape and letting her pass. "Watch out for those media animals. They'd steal the pizza outta your mouth and the hat off your head if you gave them half a chance."

"Tell me about it," Zoe said, and strolled into the apartment building.

When the grieving parents opened the door—clutching their one surviving child in diapers between them—Zoe called upon her high school Spanish to tell them she worked for *The Trumpet.*

"¡Oh sí! *La Trompeta*," the mother said, looking to Zoe for some kind of justice.

Between her very limited English and Zoe's rusty Spanish, they worked out a deal where Zoe would help find the men who killed their sons if the parents would cooperate with her on a story.

Zoe snatched up every snapshot of the boys, making sure not to leave a single photo for any rival newspaper. Then she sat down and listened as the parents told her how police officers had been taking money to let gangs sell drugs outside the apartment building.

It was her first big story. The front-page headline above the pictures of the dead boys screamed: CROOKED COPS AND DRUG KINGS KILL KIDS!

Half a dozen police officers were arrested, several senior officers were forced to resign, and Zoe was immediately promoted to the police beat over many more senior reporters. Within a year, *New York* magazine had dubbed her "The Queen of Crime" for her relentless investigations of both criminals and cops. At 29, Zoe was at the top of her game . . . but the game had come to an abrupt end.

After being tipped off that an NYPD sergeant on medical leave was peddling drugs near a Bronx schoolyard, Zoe was convinced she had another cop-on-the-take feature. She'd found the sergeant's house and tailed him for weeks until he turned up near a schoolyard of screaming kids. She was half a block away with her camera when the sergeant exchanged packages with a man Zoe recognized as a known drug dealer with mob connections. She snapped a picture of the transaction, and could practically taste the Pulitzer Prize.

Unfortunately, she couldn't get any comment from the police department spokesperson.

Two days before the story ran, the police chief called her at home at midnight and left a message on her answering machine.

"Zoe, I'd appreciate it if you held that story until next week," the chief had asked. "We're running our own investigation, and anything in the papers right now would be a goddamn disaster. I'll explain it to you in a few months."

Yeah, right . . . a few months to cover up another bad cop, Zoe thought. *That story is running tomorrow.*

And it *did* run the next day, right across the front page. Zoe came to work early, half expecting *The New York Times* or *The Washington Post* to be calling her with job offers. But when the phone rang, it was her managing editor summoning her to his glass-enclosed office.

His chubby face was beet red, and she knew she was in serious trouble. "I'm told the police chief called you last night and asked you to hold the story. Is that right?"

"Um . . . someone called, but my answering machine isn't working. Is there . . . a problem?"

"Not really, except that your so-called dirty cop was undercover, investigating a drug ring suspected of funneling money to terrorists. But guess what? He's not doing that anymore, thanks to you. He's not a cop at *all* anymore because his picture is on the front of my goddamned newspaper!"

He stood there, struggling for breath, mopping his face with a Dunkin' Donuts napkin. "I want your resignation on my desk in an hour!" he finally spat.

"I'm not quitting. You want to fire me, then fire me. But you approved the story, and if I go, I'm taking you with me," Zoe said.

The man's face turned gray. Zoe though he was having a stroke.

"All right, Miss Crane, have it your way. Don't quit. In fact, take the rest of the day off and enjoy yourself. But be here early tomorrow for reassignment. Now get out of my sight."

The next day the receptionist directed Zoe to her cramped new cubicle across from the police-scanner room. There was a yellow self-help paperback on her desk called *Astrology for Absolute Morons*.

The book was signed by the managing editor: *All the best to a "star reporter." Copy is due Fridays—don't be late.*

A clipping from that day's lifestyles section was tucked inside the pages of the book:

> *For amusement purposes only!* The Trumpet *is happy to introduce a new feature in this section called "Your Lucky Stars." This column will keep you abreast of the latest in New Age news, as well as provide your daily horoscope, and a column from Lucky Stars reporter Zoe Crane.*
>
> *"I can't wait to get started," said Zoe. "I've been preparing for this my entire career, and now that I've got the New Age beat, I don't think I'll ever be able to leave. I'm polishing my crystal ball and counting my lucky stars!"*

Zoe sat down hard. She knew that staying on at *The Trumpet* could mean the end of her career as a serious journalist. But quitting would be a sign of weakness—and other papers wouldn't exactly be clamoring to hire her after a major front-page screwup.

She opened *Astrology for Absolute Morons* to page one and started reading. If it hadn't been for her assistant, Carolyn, she would have been completely lost. Fortunately, the young woman was obsessed with anything New Age and threw herself into research on the topic, giving Zoe time to do more investigative stories, like tracking down phony psychics.

"CENTRAL, THIS IS HARBOR 2. There's some weird stuff on this mannequin. . . ."

The scanner was buzzing again.

Zoe looked over to the cop room and saw that Sleepy and Dopey had nodded off again.

"This is Central, Harbor 2, didn't copy that . . . say again."

"There's some weird graffiti or something painted on this dummy—looks like an exploding castle or something."

"Harbor 2, don't waste time on this. Cut it loose, pull it out of the water, and get back to your post. Central out."

"Roger that, Central . . . Harbor 2 out."

Busy day on the river, Zoe thought, returning to her column and beginning to type:

Capricorn: You may have forgotten something . . .

She looked at the clock.

Oh, shoot, talk about forgetting something—I almost missed the subject of next week's column.

She turned on the radio and tuned in to WARP. The static was terrible, but as soon as the reception cleared, she could hear Katherine giving bad news to what seemed to be a very angry caller.

"I see fire all around you . . . there's smoke, I'm choking—"

"You should choke on your words, lady! You should be ashamed of yourself. Screw you and the broom you flew in on!"

Zoe laughed. But seconds later she realized there was nothing funny about what she was hearing: "Oh my God . . . oh my God! It's an explosion . . . many explosions . . . God, no . . . it looks like another attack. The explosions are going to happen here, in New York. Oh my God, it's going to happen today!"

Zoe froze, and her reporter's instincts kicked into high gear. *Holy crap, did she just predict another terrorist attack? And on national radio?*

Zoe reached under her desk for the knapsack she'd had ready ever since 9/11. It was stuffed with everything a reporter would need in the field to handle any dangerous situation—from bandages to a stun gun.

She grabbed her palmtop and ran to the elevator. *Katherine has either gone crazy, or she has some kind of inside information on a possible terrorist attack,* she thought. *Either way, I've got a major story. If I hurry, I can be at the radio station in less than five minutes.*

She was already on the street, halfway to the BioWorld Tower, when the police scanner at her office went off again. This time no one was listening.

"Central, this is Harbor 2. The wires on this dummy are . . . oh no . . . we've got fire in the hole . . . our gas tank just . . . oh my God, there's a . . ."

There was a sharp burst of static, and then the scanner went silent.

CHAPTER 5

FRANK DELL KICKED THE REAR BUMPER of his old Dodge pickup truck, and the tailgate dropped open with a heavy clang. Leaning forward, he let two 100-pound bags of fertilizer slip from his shoulders onto the truck's bed, sending a cloud of dust in the air and rattling the landscaping tools piled next to the wheel well.

It was still early, and he'd done very little heavy work, but sweat was already streaming into his eyes, and his work shirt was soaked through. He moved across the new lawn toward the company toolshed, avoiding the sun by walking through the shade cast by the bridge directly above him.

Man, she's a hot one—like being back in the freakin' desert. Everybody in the city's going to be cooked by noon . . . must be this solar storm everyone's talking about, he thought, slamming the shed door tight and securing it with a thick titanium padlock.

Frank wiped the sweat from his forehead and looked down the length of the island.

He was a tall man—well over six feet, with the tan complexion and lean, muscular build of someone who'd spent his life working outdoors. Although he was in his early 40s, his body was laced with sinewy muscle, and he moved with the confident energy of a high school athlete.

Frank bent down and stroked the tips of the boat-shaped

blades of young Kentucky bluegrass he'd laid six weeks earlier. Roosevelt Island was just over two miles long and not even a thousand feet across. He'd landscaped almost half of it, and it was by far the biggest job he'd ever tackled on his own. But the work came naturally to him. His people had worked miracles— turning parched, arid land in Sicily into rich vineyards—back when their family was still known by the name Delvecchio.

He sucked in a mouthful of air and savored the earthy aroma, taking pride in what he'd accomplished. The lawn stretched north for a mile from the ruins of the old smallpox hospital at the southern tip of the island, all the way up to below the Queensboro Bridge where it engulfed the sparkling new Supercomputer Re-Creation Center, which was scheduled to open that morning.

The landscaping was simple and, Frank thought, elegant: a few strategically placed Japanese rock gardens breaking up the sea of green; a lilac path running down the center; and a hundred cherry trees lining the asphalt walk that circled the lower half of the island. The acres of grass replaced what had been a concrete wasteland of burnt-out hospitals and crumbling laboratories, abandoned and forgotten decades ago. In the center of the lawn was a giant blue rosebush that Conrad Dinnick had personally requested.

Like the tree in the middle of Eden, Frank silently approved.

He knew he was lucky—he'd only been landscaping for six years and, really, should never have landed such a big contract. But he'd gotten a call from a former general now running BioWorld Security, who said that he needed a good man he could trust, and that Frank's Army record was "spectacular." Next thing Frank knew, he had a check for a $30,000 and the promise of $200,000 more when the whole thing was done.

When he wasn't spending time with his daughter, Samantha, he put in 20-hour shifts to finish the job on time and do it well. Not only did he need the money, but he knew that everybody in the city was going to see his work. Roosevelt Island sat smack-dab in the middle of the East River, between Manhattan and Queens, and millions of people saw it every day.

He took a deep breath and smiled. *I didn't botch it—it's gorgeous, and it's a free organic billboard advertising my handiwork to the biggest city in America.*

And God knew, Frank needed the business. The savings account was nearly dry, the advance money was nearly gone, the mortgage was overdue, and his Army pension didn't come close to covering Samantha's medical bills for the more advanced treatments she required.

He sat on the ground and yanked the mud-caked construction boots and worn-out socks from his feet. Before slipping on his sneakers, he sank his feet in the damp, lush green, enjoying the touch of a living thing against his skin after so many years spent in places of dust and death.

Oh Jesus, I'm late. I've gotta get Sam, Frank thought, checking his watch and looking up at the Queensboro Bridge while hearing the relentless honking overhead. It sounded like it was being swarmed by a flock of psychotic Canada geese, which meant that trying to cross it this morning would become a daylong nightmare.

He'd have to take a detour if he was going to get to the clinic on time. Instead of the Queensboro, he'd have to drive north and cross into Manhattan using the Triboro Bridge into East Harlem, before doubling back 40 blocks to the clinic. *That could take an extra freaking hour,* he realized, and jumped into the truck.

"FINISHING UP EARLY, FRANK?" a guard asked, when he reached the checkpoint beside the Supercomputer Re-Creation Center.

The guard leaned out of his sentry box and eyeballed the back of the truck while Frank handed over his DNA-encoded clearance card. The Island was crawling with Conrad Dinnick's brown-shirted, pseudo-cop security force today, and it gave Frank the creeps.

Sure, it's been a long time since I wore a uniform, but at least I earned the right to wear one. But these punks? Frank thought bitterly.

He couldn't stomach the sight of these rent-a-cops marching around saluting each other like a bunch of neo-Nazis. And it seemed as if they were spreading all over the city as BioWorld put up more and more buildings in New York.

"I said, you finishing up early today, Frank?" the guard repeated.

"Huh? Oh yeah, well, I actually finished the main work yesterday. Just had to make sure everything was cool before the ceremony starts this morning. Don't want the sprinklers accidentally going off and raining on the boss's parade."

"I'm sure Mr. Dinnick will appreciate that, Frank. Anyway, the grass looks good. I can't believe you landscaped half the island all by yourself," the guard said, swiping Frank's ID through a small black box and passing it back through the window.

"I guess I don't like handing out paychecks to anyone except myself. Can I go?"

"Just a sec . . . couldn't help noticing some fertilizer, quite a few rolls of sod, a rake, and few shovels in the back of your truck there. Planning on taking them off the island?"

"It's my truck, and it's my stuff. Maybe you didn't notice, but I run a landscaping company. You want to run an inventory on everything in the storage shed, go right ahead. But I don't have time to stick around waiting for it. If anything's missing, call the cops and report me. Okay, pal?"

"No need to be rude, Frank. It's my job to keep track of these things."

"Good job you got there. Now open the gate, *please,*" Frank said, not looking at the man.

"Sure, Frank, and you have a nice day now."

Frank gunned the Dodge, leaving a black patch of rubber streaked across the freshly paved road and yelled, "Sieg heil!" as he sped away.

The sleek, stainless steel walls of the Supercomputer Re-Creation Center rose steeply on his right, reflecting the morning light as it soared toward the bottom of the Queensboro

Bridge—each wall panel was engraved with a single blue rose.

A catering van was parked in front of the building, its rear door open wide to expose stacks of folding chairs and boxes of plastic-wrapped crystal champagne flutes. A string quartet was setting up on a small stage, and at least a dozen state troopers and Secret Service agents were walking bomb-sniffing dogs around the building's perimeter.

"Goddamn son-of-a-bitch no-good bastard mutts!" Frank yelled. "Those four-legged mongrels better not crap on my new lawn."

A vein over Frank's left eye began to throb, a sure sign that his blood pressure was rising fast. The brief exchange with the security guard had left him seriously aggravated, and he knew that Samantha would pick up on his stress instantly—and that would be even worse for her than if he was a little bit late.

Pulling over to the side of the road, Frank got out of the truck for a minute to do the relaxation exercises Samantha had taught him, the ones from her pain-management sessions. Breathing slowly through his nose, he let the air drop to his belly, and then he exhaled slowly from his mouth, all the while trying to visualize "a happy place." But the air by the water stank of dead fish, and the only thing he could visualize was the skyline of midtown Manhattan on the other side of the river, shimmering in the hazy smog and harsh yellow light of a too-hot New York morning.

A police boat was advancing toward the island from the middle of the river. A fat cop stood on the bow twirling a grappling hook like an overweight cowboy trying to lasso a sea cow.

Frank looked up at the century-old Queensboro Bridge—50,000 tons of intricately laced structural steel, so groovy looking that Simon and Garfunkel had written a song about it.

I can't believe the city actually sold that beautiful hunk of metal just to balance the books, he thought, as the Roosevelt Island tram came sliding alongside the top of the bridge, suspended 250 feet above the river on cables stretching from the island all the way up the wheelhouse on Second Avenue.

If I didn't have the truck, I could just jump on the tram and be in Manhattan in eight minutes, Frank thought, heading back to the Dodge.

He crossed the island and drove north on Main Street to the East Channel bridge leading to Queens. In the rearview mirror he noticed a Lincoln Town Car hard on his tail. A Town Car usually meant NYPD detectives, so he pulled over as a courtesy to let them pass.

As Frank waited for them to go by, he looked at the ruins of the notorious 19th-century lunatic asylum and remembered the day he'd brought Sarah to the island to apartment hunt. They'd been married only a year then, and he'd just finished his last tour in the Gulf. The Army had loaned him to the United Nations for a couple of years, and he'd thought the island would be a convenient and inexpensive place to live.

"It's not exactly teeming with trendy nightspots, but the rents are half what they are across the river, and I can get to the UN in 15 minutes," he'd said to Sarah.

Sarah, as usual, had done her homework and had come prepared with a binder filled with housing prices and local history.

"Nice neighborhood you've picked, Franklin Madison Dell. Just over there is where the city dumped its smallpox victims. Over here was the infamous New York City poorhouse, but that was before they built the penitentiary for the really bad-ass criminals. Here's my favorite quote from a 1930s magazine article: 'Roosevelt Island is the miserable sewer into which New York dumped its pitiful sweepings.' Oh yeah—it used to be called Welfare Island, where they put all the poor folks like us . . . and then there was the insane asylum with a long history of abuse and torture and—"

"Okay, honey, I get the point. We'll buy the house you like in Jersey."

"Thanks, Frank," Sarah had said, reaching for his hand and flattening it against her belly. "Besides, this really isn't the kind of place you want to raise your child, is it?"

"What? You're not . . . ?" Frank had asked in wonderment.

"No, Frank . . . *I'm* not. But *we* are."

THE TOWN CAR PASSED, and Frank followed it through a second checkpoint, across the bridge and into Queens.

Forty-five minutes later, he pulled up in front of the cancer clinic. It was the first time he hadn't held Samantha's hand during a chemo treatment, and he felt awful about it. But what could he do? The money from the contract meant money for more chemo and experimental drugs.

He found her in the waiting room with a nurse.

"How ya doing, slugger?"

"Just peachy keen," Samantha replied.

Frank thanked the nurse and bent to pick Samantha up.

"I'm not crippled, Frank," she said, feebly pushing his arm away. "Just carry my barf bag for me, please."

When they reached the truck, Frank opened the door and waited while Samantha struggled onto the seat. He was gently closing the door behind her when he spotted the Lincoln Town Car parked across the street. He recognized the ripped American flag flapping on the bent antenna, and knew immediately it was the same car he'd followed off the island.

That's strange, he thought, climbing behind the wheel. "So, kiddo, whaddaya say we call it a day and head home? We can pick up *The Lion King* and invite your buddies Ben and Jerry to come over."

Samantha said nothing.

"I know I promised, Sammy, but it's so hot outside and, honest, sweetie, you look . . . well . . . just a little tired."

Samantha did up her seat belt and sat quietly.

"Okay, Sam," Frank said, starting the truck. "St. Pat's or the mosque?"

"It's Friday. Take me to the mosque."

THE RITUAL MUSLIM CALL TO PRAYER wailed from the towering minaret of Manhattan's largest mosque at Third Avenue and

96th Street. It was the official prayer time, and the plaintive, beckoning cry echoed down the street.

"They're calling me, Franklin. I've got to go."

Frank looked at his 11-year-old daughter pulling impatiently on the passenger door's long silver lever. He knew that she only used his full first name when she was mad at him. He figured she was pissed off because he'd been late getting to the clinic. He didn't blame her; he was pissed at himself.

They'd been going through the same routine every Tuesday and Friday for months: a 45-minute drive from their home across the Hudson River in Newark, then an hour to 90 minutes at the clinic. Afterward, unless Samantha was really sick, they'd stop at St. Patrick's Cathedral so she could say a prayer and light a candle for her mom; or a make a prayer trip to a temple, synagogue, or mosque before taking the tunnel back beneath the river and heading home.

Frank had long ago accepted Samantha's strange fascination with world religions, even though he hadn't set foot in any house of worship since Sarah had been killed. But his daughter insisted that he wait outside wherever and whenever she was struck by the mood to pray. And lately, the mood was striking her more and more often.

He wasn't sure when it had started, but he guessed it had been the second-to-last Christmas Eve that Sarah had been alive. His wife had tried to explain the concept of Santa Claus to Samantha, but, being a Muslim, she had a hard time herself with the story of St. Nick.

"He has a magic moose that pulls him in a big wagon across the sky right around the whole planet, and they stop on rooftops while he jumps down chimneys and puts presents under potted plants for all the girls and boys in the world," Sarah had explained hesitantly, looking at Frank for support, but getting none.

"And Santa Claus is supposed to do this in one night? Fuhgettaboutit!" Samantha had responded, cracking both of them up. Even at five, she'd been precocious, with a wickedly wry sense of humor, an insatiable curiosity, and a phenomenal memory. She never forgot a single detail of anything she heard, no matter how minute or insignificant. She'd dismissed the Santa story out of hand, and for the rest of that Christmas Eve, the three of them had sat around wrapping presents, drinking cocoa, and discussing the many religious beliefs held by people from different cultures.

Frank remembered that after that night, Samantha couldn't get enough of religion. There were mandatory Bible readings at bedtime as well as stories from the Torah and Koran. Later, she insisted on hearing tales from Greek mythology, and was enthralled by the bloody battles waged by the Hindu gods.

Samantha's Beach House Barbie set became a surreal Nativity scene where the baby Jesus had a big brother named Buddha, and Ken and Barbie took everyone to Mecca for picnics. For the next two years, Samantha insisted that her mother accompany her to the mosque every Friday, and that Frank take her to Mass every Sunday. She made both of her parents wait for her outside the temple on Saturdays.

"She's one really weird kid, Sarah. Maybe we should take her to a shrink. Did you ever know any kid who wanted to go to church even once a week, much less two or three times?" Frank had asked Sarah while they waited for Samantha's Bible study class to finish one Sunday afternoon, a month before Sarah left.

"Come on, Frank. She's just curious . . . and so smart it's scary. Do you know that she can recite the names of all the books of the Bible, quote from the Koran, and rattle off the names and special powers of every god on Mount Olympus? She's remarkable, not weird, and she's having fun. I think we should just let her explore. Besides, think of all the money you're saving in ballet lessons."

"That's what I mean. Little girls usually want to be ballerinas, but our kid wants to be Pope or something. I don't even think she really believes half the stuff she reads."

"She's developing her own beliefs, and that's really special—particularly at her age." Sarah had moved close to him and leaned her head against his shoulder.

"You know what she said to me when I tucked her in last night?" she continued. "That she thought different religions are just different languages people speak in heaven, and she had to learn all of them in case God needed to speak to her one day. She calls it 'God language.' Doesn't that break your heart?"

"No, Sarah, what breaks my heart is you going back to that hellhole."

"Please . . . don't start. It's only for two weeks. It's not like there's an oversupply of Arab-speaking aid workers. You know how many orphans are over there now?"

"We've got our own daughter to take care of, and we both served our time. How much more do we have to give?"

"Please, Frank . . ."

"Sarah, I've got a bad feeling about this."

"I promise I'll be extra, extra careful. Besides, I'm going to be with the good guys, remember?"

"Okay . . . okay. Just be back for Easter. Sam's got her heart set on you seeing her in the Sunday-School pageant."

"I promise. Nothing could keep me away."

NOTHING BUT A BLOODTHIRSTY GRUNT WITH AN M16, Frank thought.

At Sarah's funeral, Frank dropped the crucifix his mother had given him into the coffin.

"Daddy, didn't Nonna give that to you? Why are you giving it to Mommy?" Samantha had asked him, as they left the cemetery.

"I don't need it anymore. I don't want it anymore. I don't believe in any of it anymore."

The continuing call to prayer jolted him back to the present. Samantha was sitting beside him, fighting with the door handle.

In the four years since Sarah's death, Frank had tried to make sure that Samantha never missed her prayer sessions. Even sickness hadn't curbed her enthusiasm, and he figured that her passion was good medicine as long as it didn't tire her out too much. So far it hadn't, but watching her wage a losing battle with the door handle made him think that it was time for her to slow down.

"Oh, stop looking so worried, Daddy. I'll get it . . . eventually," Samantha said, looking at her father and hitting the lever with a balled-up fist.

Frank studied her face. The warm olive complexion she'd inherited from her mother had been dulled by the chemo, leaving her looking chalky. The dark circles under her eyes and the red kerchief she wore to hide her vanished dark curls gave her the look of a seasick pirate. But as ill as she was, Frank knew that she could turn on a thousand-watt smile if she was happy. And it didn't take much to please her: a favorite song on the radio, a sweet story about her mother, a dish of Chunky Monkey ice cream. . . .

But she wasn't smiling this morning; she wasn't at all pleased with Frank. And he soon realized that it had nothing to do with his being late.

"Let me help you," he offered, leaning over to open the door.

"I don't need your help."

"I just want to—"

"I know what you want, Daddy, but you can't have it."

"I don't know what you're talking about, Sammy."

"Yes, you do, Daddy."

"I don't."

"You're lying. You promised you would never lie to me, and now you lie all the time. You're a liar, Franklin."

"I'm not . . . I . . . if it's the chemo . . . you know you have to have the treatments."

"Why? They just make me sicker. They make me throw up, and they make me bald."

"I know they do, sweetheart, but you know you need them to get better."

"I'm not stupid, Frank. *I* know I'm not going to get better, and *you* know I'm not going to get better. So stop lying to me, and stop lying to yourself. I'm dying."

"Don't ever say that."

"But it's the truth."

"Don't say it."

"It's true."

Frank stopped talking. He stared at his daughter, who was gazing out the window into the courtyard of the mosque where half a dozen women and girls, their heads and faces covered, were praying quietly.

Frank and Samantha had been fighting her leukemia for two years. It went into remission but always came back. Two weeks ago, Samantha's oncologist told Frank that they'd done everything they could do for her, that even with continued chemo and the newer, more expensive drugs, all they could hope to do now was keep her comfortable. The doctor had said there was little chance she'd survive the year, and suggested that the most humane thing to do would be to end the chemo and let Samantha enjoy the time she had left.

"Very little chance doesn't mean *no* chance," Frank said to the doctor, feeling like he wanted to snap the man's neck in two. Later, he told Samantha that the cancer was going away, but the doctors said it would just take longer than expected. They had to be brave and keep up with the treatments. Samantha had given him a quizzical look and said, "Okay, Daddy, if that's what you think is best."

But today Samantha looked more exhausted than he'd ever seen her, and he wondered if he was doing the best thing for her.

"Listen, Sammy, I know I'm not good at . . . I mean, your mom—"

The call to prayer was playing again.

"It's okay, Daddy, don't worry about it. We'll talk later, all right? But I've got to go."

Samantha gritted her teeth and pulled up on the lever with all her strength. The door popped open. Frank leaned over, placing his hand gently on his daughter's arm before she slipped out of the cab.

"Hold on a second, Sammy. Allah may be great, but he's not

in such a great hurry that a little girl can't kiss her father good-bye before prayers."

He wrapped his arms around her, and she pecked him on the cheek before breaking his hug and pulling her small prayer rug from the glove compartment.

"Honestly, Daddy, I'm not going anywhere. I'll be, like, ten feet away, and you can watch me through the fence the whole time. Now I really have to go. And for God's sake, try to fix the door handle before I get back."

Frank laughed. He watched her in the rearview mirror as she entered the mosque's main gate, and then he saw it again: the Lincoln with the bent antenna and ripped flag.

Okay. Twice is a coincidence, three times is a definite tail, Frank thought.

He flipped on the truck's radio for a traffic report to plan his escape route. But what came through the speaker wasn't a traffic update—not by a long shot.

"Oh my God . . . oh my God! It's an explosion . . . many explosions . . . God, no . . . it looks like another attack. The explosions are going to happen here, in New York. Oh my God, it's going to happen today!"

Frank looked through the fence and saw Samantha spreading her prayer mat on the ground. He wasn't exactly sure what he'd just heard on the radio, but it didn't sound good—and he wasn't taking any chances where his daughter was concerned. He grabbed the door handle.

I've got to get her out of here.

CHAPTER 6

CONRAD DINNICK PULLED THE SHARP BLADE of the heavy straight razor away from his throat, glaring at the helicopter hovering in front of his window. He could tell by the color and markings that it wasn't one of his.

I build a multibillion-dollar tower and I have Peeping Toms? For God's sake . . . and today of all days! He placed the razor on the washbasin and pressed one of the many red intercom buttons scattered throughout his rambling penthouse suite at the top of the BioWorld Tower in Manhattan.

"Why is there a news helicopter outside my bedroom window?!" he demanded.

Within seconds, a voice from the building's main security desk piped through the suite's concealed speakers: "Security Chief Wilson here, sir. There seems to be some breaking news in the vicinity—a huge traffic tie-up on the Queensboro Bridge, and police activity on the river just in front of Roosevelt Island."

"Police activity in front of the island? Will this be a problem for the ceremony?" Conrad asked.

"No. No problem at all, sir. The area is secure—just a boating mishap with one of the Harbor Units. Should be cleared up shortly, but the news choppers are swarming around it like flies. I've called the NYPD Aviation Unit, and have been assured the airspace will be cleared momentarily," Wilson reported in a brisk, no-nonsense manner.

A blue and white police helicopter swung into Conrad's view as the security chief finished speaking. Conrad couldn't hear anything on the other side of the UltraPlexi window he'd personally designed to safeguard him from unwanted noise and uninvited bullets. Whatever was silently exchanged between the two aircraft was effective.

"Never mind," Conrad said, leaning on the intercom button again. "It's gone. Put another security detail on the river, and clear my bridge."

"Right away, sir . . . Wilson out."

Conrad returned to his vanity basin and continued shaving with calculated strokes. He was nearing 60, but still looked like he was in his late 40s. A recent *New York Times* profile described him as "the eternally youthful founder of BioWorld Security— a lean, mean, trillion-dollar gene machine." It attributed his vitality to his chore-filled, Iowa farm upbringing; a fastidiously healthy diet; a lifelong avoidance of tobacco, alcohol, and drugs; and a near-monkish aversion to emotional entanglements—except for, the reporter noted, one messy, highly publicized divorce.

When Conrad read the profile, he was amazed by how so-called professional journalists were so often completely ignorant about topics they were paid to write about. Yes, his marriage had ended in divorce and had made headlines because of the size of the settlement, but it wasn't messy in the least. He'd handled the divorce the way he handled everything: with clinical efficiency. He'd simply married the wrong woman—someone who couldn't accept that his work came before anything else, and who was overwhelmed by the responsibilities of motherhood.

She'd become an emotional burden, making constant demands on his time and interfering with his research, so he'd offered her $10 million in exchange for an uncontested divorce, and then she was out of his life forever.

The farm-boy anecdote was also a fabrication. The only chore expected of him was finishing library books before their due dates. As far as his looks were concerned, that wasn't about clean living, it was all about good genes. That fact had been the governing truth of his life since his mother summoned him to her greenhouse on the frigid February afternoon of his eighth birthday.

"Did you know, Connie, that even a simple farmer's wife can play God?" his mother had asked, leaning over a shrub taller than he was. "I'd like to introduce you to Miss Rosa Blanda. She's pretty enough to become Iowa's official state flower. But like lots of pretty things, she's weak, Connie." She cupped one of the plant's soft, pink flowers in her hand and inserted a pair of tweezers in its center.

"All I have to do is borrow a few cells from pretty Miss Rosa, and I can give them to a sturdy, but less beautiful, domestic rose—and I've made a new flower that's both beautiful and strong. My own act of cosmic creation, Connie," she'd explained, dropping the wild rose's pollen into a small glass dish and handing the tweezers to Conrad.

"Here's a blue tulip and a white rose," she'd said. "It's your turn to try, Connie. If a farmer's wife can play God, I don't see why a farmer's son can't, do you?"

Conrad was brought back to the present by the sound of the sliding doors of the suite's private express elevator opening with a hiss of pressurized air, followed quickly by heavy foot-steps. A man in his mid-30s who bore a striking resemblance to Conrad lurched into the room, red-faced, breathless, and stum-bling over his words.

"Um, uh . . . oh boy. On the radio, on the radio, yeah," the man blurted out, staring at his shoes and sucking air noisily through his mouth.

Conrad looked at him, and, as always, was amazed at the difference in temperament and bearing between his two sons—considering they'd been born identical twins, and it had been utterly impossible to distinguish one from the other physically.

His colleagues at the time had dubbed Conrad "The Godfather" when Michael and Daniel were born because monozygotic—identical—twins were often referred to as God's clones since they shared an identical DNA code.

What were the odds, they'd joked, *of a geneticist specializing in gene replication producing identical twins?* Well, he knew the odds—they were the same as for everyone else—one in 285, not a long shot by any stretch, but long enough to start a whisper campaign that he'd been taking his work home with him.

Conrad also knew that, statistically, the boys should share similar IQs and personality traits. But while the boys *looked* the same, they'd turned out as different as night and day.

From the time he could speak, Michael exuded a natural poise and remarkable self-confidence. By the end of high school, he'd mastered three languages, and eventually became the youngest-ever recipient of a Ph.D. from Stanford's genetics program. He'd joined the family business as a BioWorld Security senior vice president before he turned 26.

Michael had inherited Conrad's passion for science, but his ambition to always be first, combined with a ruthless intellect, had worried his father immensely.

While Conrad was undoubtedly the most daring scientist of *his* generation, he was always deliberate and careful in his experimentation. Michael's approach, however, made his father look like a timid schoolboy. Despite everyone's acknowledgment of his brilliance, Michael seemed driven to outdo Conrad's breakthroughs, and was often extremely reckless in his research, dismissing both safety and ethical issues in his pursuit of results.

That recklessness had caused a major rift between father and son after Conrad discovered that the young man was injecting himself with a large number of stem cells extracted from hundreds of human embryos, which was not only incredibly dangerous, but also illegal.

They fought bitterly—a vicious argument that echoed through the complex. Conrad accused Michael of jeopardizing his government contracts as well as the funds he received to search for cures for a dozen diseases from Alzheimer's to multiple sclerosis.

At first Michael seemed hurt, yelling at his father, "You've never picked on Danny like this! You've always let him do whatever he wanted, no questions asked. All I've done my entire life is try to please you, to show you how much I respected your work, to advance your research . . . but you do nothing but criticize me. Nothing will ever satisfy you unless you can do it yourself and claim the glory as all your own—isn't that right, Dad? So I took a few embryos and used some stem cells for my research. So what? You've made a fortune selling human growth hormone to people afraid of getting old and tired. What's the difference?"

Then Michael laughed in Conrad's face. He lashed out at his father, accusing him of wasting his life trying to "cure" disease—and that the real challenge was to beat death altogether . . . to stop the aging process by preventing human cells from decaying.

"I'm not talking about using Botox to smooth out wrinkles on middle-aged ladies, or developing a new kind of chemotherapy to squeeze a few more years of life into the sick and dying!" Michael screamed. "I'm taking about *real* eternal youth—about conquering death. You've always played at being God, Dad. I'm going to *be* God!"

Conrad had realized at that moment that his son—either through the experimental drugs he'd injected or because of insanely out-of-control ambition—had become unstable, and a dangerous liability to BioWorld.

He banned Michael from setting foot inside the Hoboken research laboratory ever again. It was the last time he'd talked to his son. Six months later, Michael stole a gun from a BioWorld security guard and killed himself.

Conrad tried not to think about it, but it was nearly impossible not to when Daniel was standing in front of him looking exactly like Michael, but acting as though he'd crawled out of a completely different gene pool.

Daniel was sweating profusely, as pathologically shy and as nervous as ever: a flushed-faced stutterer who, despite years of study at Harvard Divinity School, struggled to put a sentence together. He'd dropped out before getting his doctorate, seeming more interested in volunteering as a missionary in every backwater village of the developing world than in getting a real job. It had always irked Conrad that while Michael, despite his obsessiveness, was earning millions of dollars for BioWorld, Daniel was in the African bush handing out Bibles to the poor.

The brothers, although inseparable as children, had been at odds with each other since adolescence. Conrad recalled hearing one of their fierce debates when they were teens: Daniel argued in his hesitant, stammering manner that you didn't use a microscope to find God, that He could be found simply by looking inward at one's own soul. Michael dismissed his argument scornfully, saying that as soon as someone developed a better MRI machine, there'd be scientific proof that the soul was nothing but a collection of hyperactive neurons bouncing around in the brain. Michael taunted Daniel by quoting Francis Crick, the co-discoverer of DNA's double helix.

"Remember what Crick said, Danny boy: 'Your joys and your sorrows, your memories and your ambitions, your sense of personal identity and free will, are in fact no more than the behavior of a vast assembly of nerve cells and their associated molecules.' That, in a nutshell, is the definition of the human soul—the gospel according to DNA."

"The g-g-gospel of DNA, is not the gos-gospel truth. Not God's truth. Everyone has a s-s-soul, Mike . . . even you . . . even Dad," Daniel would stutter back.

After Michael's suicide, Daniel seemed to change. He'd begged for a public-relations job at the BioWorld research center in Hoboken. Conrad gladly gave it to him, hoping it would force the boy to confront his shyness. But he also insisted that Daniel manage his latest acquisition—New York City's leading radio station—so he'd develop business skills to prepare him to take charge of BioWorld one day. But so far, he'd been completely inept at managing the station.

Looking at his son now, Conrad wondered in despair, *How could he come in here and disturb me while I'm preparing for one of the biggest announcements I've ever made?* Aloud, he demanded, "For God's sake, Daniel, if you've got something to say to me, spit it out! Has it slipped your mind what a critically important day this is for us?"

"No, sir, I haven't forgotten. It's a big d-d-day, sure, I know that all right, but, uh . . . there's a pro-prob-problem on the morning show."

"What kind of problem, Danny?"

"A guest, a psychic. She's saying things, things . . . she's sc-scaring people. We've had complaints . . . the police called and—"

"The *police*. Oh my God, Danny, how could you let this happen? And how did a *psychic* get booked on the show in the first place? You know how I feel about those sorts of quacks. But that doesn't matter right now. For God's sake, I made you station manager, didn't I? Go manage. Start doing your job. I've got the governor and the mayor arriving shortly, so please, no psychics and no police, okay?"

"I think you'd better come down and—"

"No, Danny. I think you'd better take care of this yourself. Now, I have to get ready for the ceremony, so excuse me."

"Okay, sir . . . I'll . . . I'll . . . I'll tell Mr. Wilson . . . tha-tha-tha-," Danny stuttered while crossing over to the control console by the elevator and pushing a blue button, ". . . that I'm . . . um . . . coming down."

"Jesus, Danny, that's not the intercom, it's the damn security door in the basement—it's never supposed to be opened . . . it breaks the building's entire air lock and lets anyone stroll into the Tower. Get away from the console, and go deal with the psychic situation, please?"

What next? Conrad wondered. *First my accountants wake me up to tell me that hundreds of millions, maybe billions, of dollars seems to have been "misplaced." Then Wilson informs me there are problems on the river just before the ceremony, and now my*

dim-witted son lets me know that the police are complaining about
a psychic on my radio station.

Conrad heard the suite's doors slide shut as Danny left and turned back to the mirror. As he dabbed more shaving cream on his face, he couldn't help but see the faces of his boys in his reflection.

His sons had been so close that they used *cryptophasia*—their own secret twin language—to communicate with each other until they started school. But after their mother had left and their grandmother, who had helped raise them, died . . . the differences that would become so pronounced by adolescence had begun to appear. Michael had always thrived in school, scoring off-the-chart grades from his very first math quiz, while Daniel became more withdrawn, began stuttering, and was reading the Bible more often than his textbooks.

But that was one of the many things about his sons Conrad hadn't known at the time—when they were young, he was far too busy conducting research for other people to worry about raising children. He let his mother and a long line of nannies attend to the child rearing. By the time the boys were teenagers, he was completely dedicated to building his own company and rarely saw them except on scheduled holidays and the occasional birthday.

Conrad finished shaving and wiped his razor clean on a hand towel before studying it in the sunlight flooding through the wraparound floor-to-ceiling windows. Daylight slid along the handle like a bubble of yellow liquid. It was 24-karat, as pure a gold as you could find anywhere on the planet. The chairman of the New York Stock Exchange had presented it to him as a gift the day BioWorld Security went public. The blade was engraved on both sides. On one side, it said: "Remember the Golden Rule of Commerce." On the other side was: "Cut their throat before they cut yours."

"If you think commerce is cutthroat, get a job as a scientist," Conrad had said as he was accepting the gift. "They'll pick your brains, your pockets, and your bones until there's nothing left to pick . . . and then pick some more."

Conrad Dinnick turned his back on pure research decades ago, not intending to use his intellect to make pharmaceutical executives rich. He invested a small inheritance to set up his first lab, and became a maverick pioneer in genetic research.

But he hadn't gone into genetics to get rich—he did it to save his mother's life. She'd been diagnosed with multiple neuronal degeneration just after he graduated from medical school. He was stunned by the diagnosis, knowing that the disease would slowly but surely destroy his mother's keen mind and leave her once-vigorous body a twisted, withered ruin. Doctors believed that the disease was caused by a genetically mutated virus, so Conrad decided to abandon a career in medicine to devote himself to finding the viral gene attacking his mother's brain and nervous system.

He never succeeded, and considered it his greatest failure—at least until Michael's suicide.

While the gene that caused his mother's illness had eluded him, it led him deep into the field of genetic research and unraveling the mysteries of DNA's double helix.

His groundbreaking work had earned him two Nobel Prizes and caught the attention of the Pentagon, and he was asked to advise the President on defending the country against biological attack. His contacts with the government soon brought lucrative contracts to his small but growing company.

Then came the first World Trade Center attack in 1993, and the beginnings of his enormous financial empire. After the bombing, he dedicated his biogenetic and computer research to national defense, developing a screening device capable of analyzing a person's entire genetic profile in a matter of seconds and downloading the information into a central database.

When the World Trade Center was attacked a second time, Conrad quietly sold several hundred Dinnick DNA Samplers to the new Department of Homeland Security—the first of dozens of his patented biotechnical devices purchased by increasingly nervous world governments.

On the fourth anniversary of the 9/11 attacks, one of Conrad's inventions detected a large quantity of aerosol anthrax in a shipping container in Calais, France. When the media reported that the discovery had probably saved hundreds of thousands of lives, the price of BioWorld Security stock quadrupled overnight and kept going up. The profits were staggering, allowing Conrad to build dozens of new research facilities, invest billions in an antiviral drug program, and develop new computer systems to help identify genetic diseases. And all the while, the profits kept pouring in.

This morning he would announce the beginning of Project PAT, BioWorld's most closely guarded, and by far, most revolutionary, venture. PAT was a method of genetic cloning that, with the aid of a massive supercomputer, would soon allow him to create—to actually grow—human organs in a laboratory. It meant that, for a certain price, no one would ever have to wait for a transplant again.

The implications would shock the world: Life expectancy in the Western Hemisphere could increase by 10, perhaps as much as 20 or even 30 years . . . and that was just the beginning. Even *he* didn't know where the research would lead once the project was up and running—the potential for putting an end to scores of genetic diseases in just a few years was within reach.

Conrad looked out of the suite's east window as he slipped into the shirt he'd had made especially for today. From the Tower's 120th floor, he had an unimpeded view of the East River and Roosevelt Island, where the new jewel of his growing empire, The BioWorld Supercomputer Re-Creation Center, or, as he simply called it, The Re-Creation Center, was about to officially open.

The cigar-shaped building stretched for more than 300 feet along the center of the skinny island. The Queensboro Bridge hovered high above, intersecting it in a way that gave the Center—at least from Conrad's bird's-eye view—the look of a giant cross.

He smiled as the morning sun flashed across the solar

panels on the building's roof—like a beacon pointing to a new future.

Just as it should, Conrad thought, knowing that inside the center was a revolutionary computer system that had the potential to rewrite every religious, philosophical, and scientific notion humankind had ever held dear.

He'd spent hundreds of billions of dollars to buy both Roosevelt Island and the famous bridge so he could build in the heart of New York—a show of support for a city still sitting at the top of the terrorist hit list.

But after today, maybe, just maybe, terrorism would no longer be such a constant threat. If Project PAT went according to plan, there would be so much less suffering in the world, so much more hope, and so much less to fight about.

He would still make immense profits from the project, but it would also be his way of giving something back.

Soon, Conrad would be joining the mayor and governor to ride the cable car down to the island. He would officially open the Re-Creation Center with a ribbon-cutting ceremony and then reveal to the world the full potential of Project PAT.

He put on his jacket, removed a carefully folded sheet of calligraphy paper from his inside breast pocket, and began to read:

"Gentlemen, ladies, honored guests, scientists, citizens of New York, and people of the world . . ." Conrad put the paper back in his pocket—he didn't need it. He looked into the mirror and rehearsed his speech.

"Two years ago I lost my son Michael, who took his life rather than die a slow, painful death brought on by an incurable disease. Today, thanks in large part to his tireless and daring research, I have the honor and privilege to announce that many who now suffer from so-called incurable diseases need no longer fear death. Today, I am proud to announce that death has been dealt a blow—"

"Excuse me, sir . . ."

"What is it now, Wilson?" Conrad said, turning toward his ceiling speakers.

"There's a woman on the radio claiming the city is about to be attacked by terrorists."

"What? I told Daniel to take care of this."

"Daniel went to the basement to check on the security door he said he accidentally opened from your suite. I would have attended to the matter myself, but I was busy dispatching additional security personnel to the island per your instructions, sir."

"Replay the radio program up here."

"Stand by, sir."

To his dismay, Conrad heard a woman's voice say: *"Oh my God . . . oh my God! It's an explosion . . . many explosions . . . God, no . . . it looks like another attack . . . ."*

A few seconds later, Conrad was tripping over his pants, trying to pull them up as he got into his private elevator. He was certain that the voice he was hearing was either an actress hired by a competitor to undermine his announcement today, or someone in cahoots with a terrorist group trying to steal his work.

He listened to the rest of the broadcast through the elevator speakers as he began the 120-floor descent to the lobby.

"The explosions are going to happen here, in New York. Oh my God, it's going to happen today!"

CHAPTER 7

KATHERINE WAS SUSPENDED IN MIDAIR, stretched out in a hammock, swinging between two poplar trees by the beach house of her dear friend Julia.

She could hear snatches of Julia's favorite Sinatra song drifting on the breeze, and she began singing along to herself.

The summer wind . . . came blowin' in . . . from across the sea . . .

The song stopped abruptly as a voice called out, "Kathy, go find Frankie's place."

Katherine sat up in the hammock, startled. She saw Julia walking toward her.

"This isn't the best time or place for a visit, Katherine," Julia said in her soft, cultivated voice.

"Julia! What am I . . . what are *we* doing here? Am I—?"

"No, Kathy, just sleeping . . . sleeping when you should be up and moving. Remember when I told you that you had a mission in store for you? Well, it's here. It's time for you to begin your journey."

"What are you talking about, Julia? Why did you bring me here?"

"I didn't bring you here. You came to me, and you have to find the answers. Go find Frankie. Drive to Sinatra. I have to go."

"Wait. I miss you so much," Katherine begged, reaching up to touch Julia's cheek.

"I miss you too, Kathy. But you have work to do. You don't want people looking like *this*, do you?"

Katherine recoiled in horror. Julia's beautiful, delicate face was filling up with open, weeping sores, and it seemed like her face was melting off her bones.

"Drive to Sinatra, or everyone could look like this," Julia said. "Now wake up . . . wake up . . . wake up. . . ."

Katherine opened her eyes, and for some reason she thought she saw an image of Abraham Lincoln above her . . . and then Tarzan's face came into view, and he was yelling: "Wake up, wake up . . . wake up!"

Pain shot through Katherine's skull as her headache returned in full force.

"Are you having some kind of mental breakdown?" Tarzan demanded, shaking his head. "Do you know the trouble we're in?" He was prancing around the room like his feet were on fire.

"What happened? What's going on here?" Katherine asked, slowly getting up off the floor and drawing herself up to her full height. She looked down at Tarzan, who quickly retreated backward a few steps.

"That's a question a lot of people, including the police and the FBI, will be asking *you*, Ms. Haywood."

Katherine whirled around and came face-to-face with a tall, blond man wearing what appeared to be an SS uniform. She rubbed her eyes and steadied herself again. She realized that the man was actually wearing an expensive, well-tailored black suit.

"Okay, please just give me a second," she said, taking a deep breath and surveying the tiny studio. There were several people in the little room, all staring at her like she had six heads.

Bronwyn, the production assistant, came running into the room and gave Katherine a glass of cold water.

"Are you okay, Katherine? You passed out."

"I . . . I think so. I don't really remember anything after the first caller. Maybe I'm still jet-lagged. I've only passed out one other time in my life."

"Well, the phones are jammed. There are a lot of freaked-out people wondering what's going on," said Bronwyn.

"Oh my God! And you don't remember what happened?!" Tarzan pressed Katherine. "Well, let me refresh your memory. You basically announced—*on my show*—that New York City is going to be attacked by terrorists today. Do you know what the FCC could do to me? I could get pulled off the air!"

"Please lower your voice," Katherine said evenly. "My head is hurting. I'm sure it will all come back to me in a few minutes. I apologize if I've disrupted your show."

"Disrupted?! We had to pull the plug on you. My show was putting out nothing but dead air for 30 seconds—*dead air!* That's the kiss of death in radio."

Katherine was trying to regain her bearings and recall the last few minutes. A second later, the images from her last readings came back to her in a flash: the red ski lift, car wrecks, a burning bridge, a collapsing tunnel . . . a uniform and a gun.

"Look, I'm sorry about what just happened here," she repeated, looking at the apprehensive faces surrounding her. "I'm as upset about it as any of you. The last thing I want to do is frighten anyone during a reading. What I said just came out, and it's—"

"'Sorry' isn't going to cut it here, lady!" Tarzan's voice was rising.

"Please, Tarzan, I'm trying to tell you that what I saw was real. Surely if your producers invited me on your show, they don't think I'm faking all of this, right? Now, I have to figure this out because someone's in trouble. Something bad is going to happen, and it's connected to this place . . . to the man on the phone. If you could just forget the show for a minute and—"

"Forget the show? It's *my* show! I'm Tarzan—"

"Shut up and sit down, Tarzan. She's right—this isn't about you," the tall blond man interjected.

"No, this *is* about me. *The Jungle Hour* has a reputation—"

"If you don't sit down, I *will* make it about you. And trust me, that's something you don't want. Do we understand each other?" the blond man asked menacingly.

Tarzan sat down behind his microphone, and the man turned to Katherine.

"Now, Ms. Haywood, let's have a little chat, shall we? My name is John Wilson. I'm chief of security for all the BioWorld facilities, including the BioWorld Tower. There have been a lot of calls coming in from local, state, and federal law enforcement regarding your statements about a possible attack on New York. Besides panicking thousands of our listeners, your little performance has upset a lot of high-ranking officials from the local police chief to the Department of Homeland Security in Washington," Wilson said.

"'Performance'?" Katherine asked, shaking her head. "You think that was some kind of act I was putting on? I would never deliberately panic people. I'm a professional, and what I said could very well be a warning to—"

"That's all well and good," Wilson interrupted, "and I'm sure your credentials are impeccable. Unfortunately, we're preparing for a rather sensitive, high-security ceremony. You've jeopardized that, and I need to find out why. So if you would please join me and my employers in the security office across the main lobby—"

"What? Are you placing me under arrest?"

"No, although I could. At the moment, I'm leaving that up to the police. I'm merely inviting you to join me in a discussion."

Katherine felt extremely uneasy about this man, but she knew that a line had been crossed, and she had to make things right.

"Okay, as long as you're asking politely, take me to see them. I'll be glad to provide an explanation," Katherine said, hoping she'd be able to clear everything up.

Bronwyn popped her head through the door to say, "We're going back on the air in 30 seconds. You'll have to clear the studio. Are you good to go, Tarzan?"

"I'm a professional—I'm always good to go," Tarzan spat, putting on his headphones and glaring at Katherine as she turned to leave.

He leaned in front of his microphone and was back in character.

"*AhhhhEEEEeeee AhhhhEEEEeeeee Ahhhhhhhh!* Hello, folks, it's Tarzan swinging back to you in the Jungle. Sorry about that little interruption. That was just a bad joke . . . nothing to worry about. This solar storm is really playing havoc with all our systems, and our guest psychic was feeling under the weather, but I think we've got things sorted out now. So whaddaya say we cool down those solar flares with a hip-hop version of an oldie but goodie—a tune made famous by the hippest cat to ever cross the Lincoln Tunnel, Hoboken's favorite son, Ol' Blue Eyes himself, my man . . . Frankie S."

Katherine stopped in her tracks. "Julia," she whispered, as Tarzan pushed the play button and the familiar words filled the suite.

"*The summer wind . . . came blowin' in . . . from across the sea. . . .*"

CHAPTER 8

ZOE LOOKED UP, WAY UP. She wasn't usually impressed by buildings, but, as always, the BioWorld Tower wowed her completely.

She'd sprinted the two blocks from her office to the Tower, hoping to get to the psychic before the police or other reporters did, but she couldn't resist pausing for a second to admire the imposing structure.

Talk about your phallic symbols! Zoe joked to herself as she strained her neck to take in the full view.

It was an intimidating skyscraper, even by New York City standards. The cylindrical ebony pillar dominated the Manhattan skyline with its dizzying height, shrouding the surrounding buildings in perpetual shadow. It had been unveiled with great fanfare and, at the time, was hailed as the *Titanic* of architecture: enormous, inspiring, and indestructible.

The Tower's revolutionary "steeltanium" frame was encased in thousands of shatterproof black windows that seemed to suck the sunlight out of the midtown area.

At the ribbon cutting, the Japanese architect had boasted that the Tower was terrorist-proof: "Hermetically sealed, with its own pure air supply, and so strong that a 747 would bounce off it like a tennis ball," although a *New York Times* columnist later wrote that the allusion was in such bad taste that something must have been lost in the translation.

Critics had dubbed Conrad Dinnick the "Prince of Darkness" for his eerie ability to convert human genome research into staggering profits. And they christened his building "The Dark Fortress"—declaring that its lack of charm was surpassed only by its radiant bleakness.

This sucker must run a mile straight up, Zoe observed, mounting the black marble steps leading from York Avenue to the Tower's main entrance.

The massive revolving door was flanked by hand-carved crystalline sculptures of the double helix—the basic structure of DNA and the foundation of Conrad Dinnick's vast fortune.

Inside, the many government offices and science labs were constructed along the perimeter of the circular walls. Each level was stacked atop the next like an upright roll of Life-Savers.

In the center of the building, a vast atrium overflowed with exotic trees, plants, and flowers that Zoe didn't recognize, and was alive with the sound of babbling streams and waterfalls. Sun filtered down through the entire atrium from a massive domed skylight 120 floors overhead.

What is this, the Amazon rain forest? Zoe couldn't believe that she'd worked down the street from the Tower for years and had never been inside. Then again, given her reputation, she wasn't on many of the city's invitation lists.

Zoe approached the main gate cautiously. Some members of Conrad Dinnick's enormous security staff were former NYPD officers, and her exposés on dirty cops had left her few fans on the police force. In general, pretty much everyone considered *The Trumpet*'s reporters to be gutter slime.

"Your business in Dinnick Tower today, Miss?" asked the guard at the security desk.

"New York Department of Environmental Health. I'll be testing for air quality today," Zoe said, offering him a fake photo ID that she'd recently paid a grand for. Since the increase in anthrax attacks, ricin scares, and dirty-bomb threats, a DEH identification card got her past most government and civilian checkpoints.

"There's nothing on the computer about a DEH inspection today, Miss . . . uh . . . Miss . . . " The officer squinted at his computer screen and then back at Zoe's fake ID.

"Merryfield," Zoe said. "Isobel Merryfield. And if you don't mind, it's *Ms*. Please check your new DEH regulation guide: chapter 7, subsection 3. You'll discover that state law grants DEH inspectors immediate and unlimited access to all buildings, structures, and substructures within New York City and surrounding counties."

"I'm familiar with the law, Ms. Merryfield, but I still don't see your name on the computer. You'll have to stick your finger in the Sampler."

"Stick my *what, where?*"

"Your finger in the Sampler, please. I have to code you."

Zoe knew about the Dinnick Sampler, but had never been asked to submit to one. The machines looked like electric pencil sharpeners, and painlessly extracted a microscopic skin sample from the user's forefinger. DNA from the sample was then recorded and downloaded into a global network that scanned for infectious diseases, drug use, and contact with restricted chemicals or pathogens. Despite civil rights protests, the Samplers were becoming more commonplace in airports, government offices, and private businesses.

Welcome to the new world, Zoe thought ruefully. She could see the red neon sign of WARP Radio flickering through the leaves from the other side of the atrium.

"Let's go, Miss. The machine won't bite, and it's a busy day."

Zoe held up her middle finger. "Is this the one you want?"

The officer sighed. "Very original. What is this, your first day on the job? Just insert your finger, please."

Zoe scowled, but then slipped her finger into the opening and felt a tiny jolt, less than a static electricity shock. Five seconds later, a green light flashed, and an electronic female voice announced: "Subject: Unknown. Status: Clean."

"What does that mean? It knows I had a shower this morning?"

"No, *Ms.* Merryfield," said the guard, rolling his eyes. "Clean means you're disease free and haven't handled things that could go boom, and now your genetic code is in the global DNA database. Just place your knapsack on the x-ray belt, and you'll be good to go."

"My bag?"

"Yes, your bag."

"Um . . . there's sensitive testing equipment in here. I'll just carry it through."

"Hand it to me, please. I'll do a physical inspection to make sure there are no—"

Across the atrium, an angry voice from the radio studio was getting louder, echoing through the cavernous atrium.

"You basically announced—*on my show*—that New York City is going to be attacked by terrorists today. Do you know what the FCC could do to me? I could get pulled off the air!"

The guard went pale and he whipped his walkie-talkie from his belt, turning his back to Zoe: "Building alert: possible Code Red. Building alert . . ."

That was Tarzan ranting, Zoe realized. *And no doubt Katherine is at the other end of it. I've gotta get in there.*

She scooped up her bag, slid it across her shoulder, and slipped into the tangle of leaves.

CHAPTER 9

CONRAD DINNICK USED THE 120-FLOOR DESCENT from his penthouse to finish dressing. He was straightening his Italian silk tie when he stepped from the private elevator and saw his son standing in the lobby.

"Danny? What the hell are you doing here? You were supposed to deal with . . . forget about it, just follow me," he snapped, brushing past his son to the Tower's west-side security desk.

"Mr. Dinnick, sir," said the guard, "the main security desk is reporting some trouble in the radio studio. A possible Code Red—"

"I know," Conrad said, sticking his forefinger into a Sampler. The machine's electronic voice stated: "Subject: Dinnick, Conrad. Status: Clean." Conrad walked through the security gate.

"But, sir . . . a possible Code Red. Should we evacuate the—"

"No! Do you want to create a panic? Do nothing until you receive a direct order from Chief Wilson or myself. Understood?"

"Yes, sir."

Conrad waited for his son to be screened by the Sampler.

"Subject: Dinnick, Daniel. Status: Clean. Subject: Dinnick, Michael. Status: Clean."

Conrad's stomach tightened as the computer announced Michael's name. As identical twins, Daniel and Michael had identical DNA, and the sampler couldn't differentiate between them. Michael had been dead for nearly two years, but Conrad hadn't had the heart to erase all traces of his son, however misguided Michael had been.

"Come on, Danny, let's get to the studio before someone calls the bomb squad."

"But s-sir, the time. I think you sh-should—"

"Should *what,* Danny?

"Get to the tr-tr-tram."

"Of course that's what I *should* do, Danny. The mayor and the governor are waiting. But once again, I'm left to clean up your mess. And this time, it's a *hell* of a mess, isn't it? The tram will have to wait."

"I'm sorry, sir, b-b-but—"

"But what? Jesus! Why couldn't you be more like your brother? Every time I give you some responsibility, you completely screw it up. At least when Michael screwed up, he was trying to make history. You screw up booking guests on a radio show, for Christ's sake."

"Bu-bu-but . . . I . . . I—"

"Enough! We've got no time. You've jeopardized Project PAT and possibly created a citywide panic. Either way, you've allowed someone to sabotage BioWorld, and now I'm going to find out if it was deliberate or accidental," Conrad stated emphatically, walking into the atrium and past a rosebush bursting with the enormous blue flower he and his mother had created for themselves so many years ago.

Daniel trailed behind him, trying to keep up.

"But D-D-Dad . . . I thought I shouldn't st-stop her because it was maybe a j-j-joke like *War of the Worlds.*"

"What the hell are you talking about? What have world wars got to do with anything?"

"No, *War of the Worlds,* Dad, sir . . . 1930s ra-ra-radio show about Mar-Martians attacking Earth. They didn't say it was pretend, and people k-k-killed themselves. I thought the psy-psy-chic, you know, would say, 'J-Just kidding, folks.'"

"'*Just kidding, folks*'? That's your reasoning, Danny? I know you're a dropout, but are you a complete imbecile?"

"I'm sorry, sir. Let me . . . f-fix it. Please, l-leave for the ceremony. The mayor, the governor, they're waiting at the tr-tr-tram for you to go to the island."

Conrad checked his watch. In a few minutes he was scheduled to ride across to Roosevelt Island with the mayor and governor to open the Supercomputer Re-Creation Center. After that, he was going to stand in front of the TV cameras and make what he knew would be one of the most monumental announcements in the history of science.

"You're absolutely right, Danny, I should leave now. But first I have to find out how much damage has been done. You take the tram and make my apologies to—"

"Oh, no . . . no! Please don't make me do that! I'm too ner-ner-nervous to—"

"For God's sake, you've got to get your act together. Today the Dinnick name will be written in the history books once again. So stand behind me, keep your mouth shut, and at least *try* to act like the heir to an empire!"

Conrad and Daniel arrived at WARP as Security Chief Wilson emerged with a tall red-haired woman wearing a white silk blouse and black tailored slacks. She looked dazed.

"Mr. Dinnick, sir, this is the psychic, Katherine Haywood," Wilson said.

"Let's cut to the chase, Miss Haywood: Whom are you working for?" Conrad demanded.

"Sinatra," Katherine said dreamily.

"What did you say?" Conrad asked.

"Frank Sinatra," she repeated.

CHAPTER 10

JACK MORGAN SNAPPED THE COVER FROM HIS MOTORCYCLE like a stage magician. And there it was, his 1969 Harley-Davidson chopper, a replica of the bike Peter Fonda had ridden as Captain America in the movie *Easy Rider*.

When Jack was a teenager, the bike had been the ultimate rebel machine. But today, the extended front forks, "ape hanger" handlebars, and Stars-and-Stripes gas tank looked ridiculously old-fashioned and silly.

But who cares what it looks like? Just get on, find that woman, and stop her lying once and for all.

Susan had loved the Harley, and while Jack hadn't sold it, he also hadn't started it since she'd died. Six or seven years ago, he'd told Mohammad across the street that he could use his garage for storage as long as he watched over the bike and kept it clean and in working order.

Jack opened the garage door, eased himself onto the seat, and with a single kick, the Harley jumped to life. He revved the engine wildly for a minute before strapping on his Captain America helmet.

The last time Jack had been in the city, the BioWorld Tower hadn't even existed, but he had no trouble finding it. Within minutes, he was speeding across the Brooklyn Bridge and could see the ugly black colossus towering over the city like a tombstone. He automatically glanced to his left, where the Twin Towers had stood, and felt like someone had punched a hole through his chest and yanked out his heart. He thought of Liam.

Don't. Just don't. Don't even think about it.

Jack headed off the bridge onto the FDR Highway and came to a dead stop. Both northbound and southbound lanes were jammed solid. He maneuvered onto the road's narrow shoulder that ran north along the East River and twisted the throttle, flying up the highway. He was almost in the BioWorld Tower's shadow when he saw flames on the river. A fire department water boat was hosing down a small blue and white cabin cruiser.

Looks like an NYPD Harbor Unit, Jack thought. *Hope none of our boys got hurt.*

Jack pulled off the highway to find police barriers blocking traffic from getting onto York Avenue. He navigated through a dozen or so demonstrators protesting in front of the Tower.

"Hey, Captain America, nice hog. But the street is closed—didn't you see the barriers? Or maybe you think the law don't apply to Easy Riders."

Jack looked at the uniformed officer walking toward him and pulled his badge from his back pocket.

"Captain Jack Morgan, *homicide.* Got someone I need to talk to inside the radio station," Jack said, looking at the Tower's marble staircase and wondering if his battered body would make it to the top.

"Jack Morgan? Get the hell outta here! You're kiddin' me, right? Jesus Christ, that's a good one . . . Crazy Jack Morgan," the officer said, laughing in Jack's face until he looked at the badge. "Holy shit, I didn't mean no disrespect, sir. Nothing like that at all. I mean, you're a legend at the academy. Best homicide close rate in department history until you . . . um . . . you know. I just thought you were like retired in Florida or something."

"I've been on special assignment, sort of low profile. Listen, will you watch my bike for a few minutes? I've got to get to this suspect before—"

"You looking for the psychic?"

"Why do you ask that?"

"Whaddaya think we got the street closed for? They're expecting a little protest 'cause of something she said that's got some people in the city spooked. Nobody tells us uniforms on the street nothing. All I know is a bunch of other shields were supposed to be heading down to talk to her, but I guess they got detoured when that Harbor Unit exploded."

"Yeah, I saw that. What happened?"

"Dunno. I hear maybe a gas line or something. They're still looking for two of our guys."

"That's rough."

"Got that right. Yeah, so I guess some of the guys are tied up over there. Plus, this traffic is just nuts. I've never seen it so bad—like everybody's trying to get out of town before noon or something, huh?"

"Yeah, it's bad all right. Watch the Harley, okay? If I'm not back in 20 minutes, the bike's yours," Jack said.

"Yeah, that's a good one, but sure, I'll watch it. Hey, Captain, I was real sorry to read about your son. That was a tough day for everyone, huh?"

"Yeah . . . a tough day," Jack said, turning toward the stairs.

"What did that psychic do to piss everyone off so much, anyway? Predict that the Mets would whip the Yankees?"

"That's exactly what she did."

"Well, she should be shot for that. Right, sir?"

"You can count on it," Jack said, slipping his hand into his jacket and gripping the handle of his .38.

He began climbing the marble stairs to the Tower.

CHAPTER 11

ZOE HURRIED TOWARD **WARP'S** FLASHING NEON SIGN. She navigated through the atrium's strange, genetically engineered foliage, hoping that by holding her tiny palmtop computer out in front of her, she looked like a busy environmental inspector.

The palmtop was a small but powerful investigative tool that had helped her bag a lot of exclusive stories. Its flip-up lid doubled as a digital video camera with a high-powered parabolic microphone capable of recording conversations from 100 feet away—just about the distance between her and the three men surrounding Katherine Haywood outside WARP's front door.

"Kaaaa-ther-innnne . . . you got some 'splainin' to do," Zoe whispered, taking cover behind what looked like a miniature palm tree. She zoomed in on the group, framing them on her little computer screen, then fished out a wireless earphone from her pocket. She popped the earphone in place, established an audio signal, and hit Record.

"Frank Sinatra?! You think this is a goddamned joke? Do you realize what you've done? The damage? The panic you've created? *Who* are you working for? Is Sinatra some kind of code name?"

Zoe didn't need to look at the screen to identify the angry voice vibrating in her ear. It belonged to Conrad Dinnick, gazillionaire genius, two-time Nobel Prize winner, presidential adviser, and at the moment, a super-pissed-off radio-station owner.

"Code name? Who do I look like, James Bond? I've told you everything I know! Please listen. This is *so important*. I think New York is going to be attacked *today!* Stop wasting time—we've got to talk to the police."

"Don't worry, lady, you'll be talking to the police. But not until I know who you're working for. So who is it? A pharmaceutical company? Al Qaeda?"

"*Al Qaeda?* What are you talking about? I'm an American citizen—and a *Democrat*. I'm not a terrorist!"

"Who then? The Syrians? Hamas? *Tell me!*"

"I'm a psychic, for God's sake. The only people I've been talking to are dead. Energies. *Spirits.*"

"So spirits told you New York was going to be attacked?" Conrad sneered at her.

"Yes, in their way, that's exactly what they did."

"And what's Frank Sinatra—chairman of the spirit board?"

"No . . . he's not related to the bombs. It's something else . . . and it's not *about* him, it's something to do with where he's *from. . . .*"

"Vegas?"

"No! Sinatra was from across the river in Hoboken. And it has to do with driving to Sinatra, or Sinatra Drive . . . I don't quite know yet. Look, we don't have much time."

"Sinatra Drive in Hoboken?" Conrad grabbed Katherine by the shoulders. "What about Sinatra Drive in Hoboken? *What are you saying?* There are bombs planted in Hoboken?"

"Stop it, you're hurting me," she tried to shake Conrad's grip. "I'm still trying to understand it myself. Julia loved Sinatra, so she used him as a reference. And maybe something about Abe Lincoln, too."

"What? Lincoln? Who's Julia? What does she know about Hoboken?" Conrad's fingers were digging into Katherine's flesh.

"Let go of me *now!*" Katherine said, pushing Conrad away. "*Just listen to me.* Julia's not in Hoboken. She's dead. She's a good friend of mine, and she's doing her best to help me, to help us all. I think she was trying to tell me that people might get sick there—*really* sick."

"Okay, this all makes sense now. A dead woman told you that people will get sick in Hoboken, right?"

"Not just with words. She *showed* me. It's one of the ways I get messages. And yes, she *said* that unless I get to Hoboken, everyone would get sick. Now, please, *please,* I'm begging you. Someone get the police right away!"

Katherine was becoming frantic. Her voice was so piercing that Zoe had to turn down the volume on her palmtop.

"Mr. Dinnick, sir, you have to get on the tram. Let me take this lady somewhere less public, somewhere I can do a thorough interrogation," said the man standing to Conrad's right.

Zoe zoomed in on the blond man with the crew cut and sleek suit. He was in head-to-toe Armani, but she could tell from his ramrod posture and severe manner that he was military through and through.

"Give me two minutes alone with her, and I'll be able to establish if she's working with someone or just a lunatic. Please sir, leave this to me," the blond man said. "You've got to get on that tram before it leaves for the island—and you better hurry. The front desk reports that there's a small group gathering outside to protest the radio show. I'll have one of my men escort you."

"That's very thoughtful, Wilson," Conrad said sarcastically. "But if you were more concerned with security and less concerned about my social calendar, I'd already be on the tram. Isn't that right, John?"

John Wilson? Zoe wondered. *General John Wilson . . . right! Former Special Forces guy in charge of finding chemical weapons in Iraq. Founder of the New Homeland Militia. He had so much power that the Army refused to fire him even after he publicly accused the White House of being weak-kneed and the Pentagon of going soft on terror. He wanted to nuke half the Middle East to get rid of terrorists. Oh yeah . . . now I really remember this winner. They called him the*

"Eye-for-an-Eye GI" because of all the Old-Testament "vengeance-is-mine" type quotes he spouted on CNN during the Iraq War. He's a certifiable Dr. Strangelove. But I thought he was still in the Army. Why's he doing BioWorld security?

"Look, sir, for your own safety, I suggest you leave for the tram now. I'll deal with our friend here," Wilson said.

"Do it, D-D-Dad . . . get on the tr-tram . . . now. Before it leaves."

Zoe adjusted the zoom again, bringing the face of the third man in the group into focus. *Well, well, if it isn't the sole heir to the BioWorld billions.* Zoe had never met Daniel Dinnick, but she'd researched him inside and out for a profile she almost wrote on the Dinnick twins.

Would have been a great story, too, if only brother Michael hadn't stuck a gun in his mouth and blown his head off, Zoe recalled, wryly remembering how her five-page feature became a half-page obituary after Michael committed suicide.

"Haven't either of you two been *listening?*" Conrad shouted at Daniel and Wilson. "This woman obviously knows about our Biosafety Level 4 lab in Hoboken. She even knows it's on Frank Sinatra Drive. And whoever she's working for also knows. So stop worrying about the stupid tram and start worrying about a nightmare scenario. I've got to get Washington on the phone. . . ."

Holy Mary . . . a Level 4 lab in Hoboken? Zoe was astounded. *If that's true, Conrad must be working with the Pentagon. How else could he be running one of the few high-security labs licensed to handle the world's deadliest viruses, from Ebola to the plague? There are only a few of those labs in the entire country—the nearest one off the coast of Long Island. But was there really one just across the river from Manhattan? Without anyone even knowing about it? Unbelievable!*

"Sir, again, let me do my job. This woman is a celebrity. She's like an actress. It's unlikely that she has any terrorist links, but I assure you, if she does, I'll find out and call Washington personally. This ceremony is so important for you, for everyone. Don't let her keep you from it—get on the tram," Wilson said to Conrad, his tone sounding almost like he was issuing an order.

"Yes, call Washington . . . call the President," Katherine pleaded. "I don't know anything about your Level 4 or 5 or whatever it is. But I do know that people are going to die unless we do something right now. I can't let this happen again, so I'm leaving. I'll find the police myself, and then I'm going to Hoboken. Abe Lincoln must mean to take the Lincoln Tunnel. See ya."

Katherine turned away, but Conrad caught her arm and spun her around. "You're not going anywhere near Hoboken. You've caused enough—"

Katherine grabbed Conrad's wrist and tried to break his grip. "That's the second time you've laid your hands on me, Mr. Dinnick. Who do you think you are? If you don't—" Katherine froze in mid-sentence. Her psychic senses were still wide-open from the radio show, and she connected with Conrad's energies as soon as she touched him.

"Wait," she said. "Stop. I'm getting someone here . . . I think it's for you." Katherine looked at Conrad. She was trying to focus on an image that was flashing in her mind of a woman. "It's a grandmother or mother energy. Definitely a mother. . . ."

Katherine's grip on Conrad tightened, and she began speaking rapidly. "Is her name Lily? She's showing me a flower. No, not a Lily . . . she's showing me a . . . is her name Rose? But I don't think that's her name . . . no, it's a blue rose. Did you and your mother grow blue roses?"

"Stop it! Just stop it!" Conrad yelled, trying to break the psychic's hold on his wrist. "You can learn everything about me and my family in a two-minute Internet search, so don't try your tricks on *me*. I'm a scientist, and at the very least, you're a charlatan and a cheat—and quite possibly an accessory to terrorism."

Katherine ignored him, speaking quickly and with increasing urgency.

"There's a son on the Other Side, your mother is bringing him through . . . they're together, and she says she met him when he crossed. Oh . . . it was violent . . . a very violent passing. Trauma to the head. It was sudden . . . like a gunshot . . . he was a Gemini? There's a strong twin energy . . . and a name . . . D-N with a long 'e' sound like Denny or Donny or maybe Danny. I'm seeing flashing red lights again. It's a warning . . . another name . . . Mac or Mick . . . no, it's Michael . . . and he's very ill. . . ."

Zoe heard the smack before she realized she'd seen it on the screen. The sound echoed across the atrium like a gunshot, so sudden and unexpected that it felt like she'd been slapped herself.

On the monitor, she saw a crimson imprint of five fingers surface on Katherine's right cheek. Blood dripped from her lip, staining her white silk blouse just above her heart.

Conrad's arm shot into the air, catching the back of his son's hand as it came swinging toward the psychic a second time.

"What are you doing, Daniel?! What's gotten into you?" Conrad asked in astonishment, his voice painfully loud in Zoe's ear. But she understood his bewilderment—the Daniel Dinnick she'd read about was a timid man, spooked by his own shadow—not the kind of guy who'd smack a woman across the face and then go at her again.

"She sh-sh-shouldn't talk about Mi-Mi-Michael like that!" Daniel gasped.

Conrad shook his head and turned to Katherine. "I apologize, Ms. Haywood. My son's behavior is inexcusable . . . but certainly understandable. I've never seen Danny raise his voice, let alone his hand to another person. But you use his radio station to spread fear and panic, and then you have the audacity to pretend to talk to his dead brother, whom he deeply loved—and his grandmother—it's too much. You've gone too far, way too far."

Katherine looked stunned. She pointed at Daniel.

"*This* is Danny?" she asked.

Conrad nodded to Wilson. Zoe heard a metallic clack and zoomed out to see that Wilson had stepped behind Katherine and handcuffed her wrists behind her back.

"Now you'll get what you want—a good, long visit with the police," Conrad said to Katherine. He turned to Wilson and Daniel as he began walking toward the security desk. "Gentlemen, let's take Ms. Haywood outside and hand her over to the authorities. I have a tram to catch."

CHAPTER 12

FRANK JUMPED FROM THE TRUCK and was running toward the mosque's courtyard when he collided with a man blocking the sidewalk.

"Whoa . . . slow down there, buddy. Where's the fire?" said the man, planting his hand firmly on Frank's chest and pushing him back several feet. The man looked to be in his early 40s and was of medium height with a wiry build, but Frank could tell from the pressure on his chest that the guy was solid muscle.

The man took one step back and placed both hands on his hips so that his jacket rode up, exposing the badge and gun clipped to his belt.

"Hey, Frank, how ya doin'?" he asked with a twisted grin.

"We know each other?" Frank asked, still feeling the effects of the shove to his rib cage. He glanced over at Samantha through the gate and saw her kneeling down.

"Sure, Frank . . . at least, I know *you*. I feel like we're old buds . . . but I guess we've never been formally introduced. Detective Kevin Christie," he said, extending his hand. Frank ignored the gesture.

"Yeah, well—Christie, is it? What do you want? I gotta get my daughter and get outta here."

"What's the big hurry, Frank? Can't we have a pleasant little chat for a couple minutes?"

This must be the goon who was driving the Lincoln Town Car that was tailing me all morning, Frank realized.

"Look, I don't know why, but you've been following me, right? Why? Did a guard on the island tell you that I stole lawn supplies? Well, I didn't, and I don't have time for bullshit, so please get outta my way. Like I said, I've gotta get my daughter."

"Come on, Frank, play nice."

"Nice? In case you didn't hear, there's been some kind of bomb threat . . . there might be a terrorist attack today. So maybe there's something else you should be doing while I get my kid away from here?"

"What bomb threat would that be, Frank?" the detective asked, his hand casually slipping to his gun.

"I just heard it on the radio."

"Really? You hear anything 'bout a bomb threat or terrorist attack, Big Davie?"

Spinning around, Frank saw a second man standing directly behind him.

"Nope," replied the other man. "You'd think they'd let us know about these things, seeing as we're on the anti-terrorism task force and all."

Frank rarely needed to look up to make eye contact with anyone, but this guy towered a good six inches over him. The man's skin was so dark that it looked blue against his white shirt. His stance was the same as the other cop, his massive right hand resting on his sidearm with a relaxed readiness. There was a shovel in his left hand, which he twirled between his thumb and forefinger as though it was as light as a pencil.

"Found this in the back of your pickup, Frank. Quite the lethal combination you've got in there: a couple hundred pounds of fertilizer, a big ol' can of gas, some coal fuel. All the fixings for an explosive little cocktail."

"Explosive? Yeah, if you're an idiot . . . and that's a $60 shovel in case you're planning to steal it," Frank said.

"Steal it? Just looking, Frank. I've developed a sudden interest in lawn care."

"This is my partner, Detective Paul Davie," Christie said. "Call him Big Davie, okay, Frank? We're all friends now, right? So what radio station did you hear that bomb threat on, Frank?"

"I don't know. I think that idiotic show with the guy who screams like Tarzan."

"*The Jungle Hour?* Hey, that's solid journalism . . . just a sec," Christie said, pulling a cell phone from his jacket pocket.

Frank looked through the fence again at Samantha, who was touching her forehead to the prayer mat. He wished he could get her attention. He had a sick feeling in his gut, and all he wanted to do was grab her and get the hell out of Manhattan. First he's accused of stealing fertilizer, then he hears someone screaming about a terrorist attack, and now two cops are shaking him down. He could taste the bile rising in his throat.

"You can stop panicking, Frank. Just talked to headquarters. You were right—there *was* a bomb threat on *The Jungle Hour,* but it's nothing to worry about. They've got some crazy psychic on the radio today making some spooky predictions. Just bullshit. The DJ already apologized, said it was all a bad joke . . . real funny, huh?"

"Yeah? Maybe it's a joke to you, but I don't take chances with my kid. If you guys really are on the anti-terrorist task force, you should know better than to dismiss any bomb threat. Now if you'll excuse me. . . ." Frank tried to move past Christie, who once again pushed Frank back, away from the gate entrance.

"Oh yeah? Guess you'd be an expert on bomb threats, Frankie," Christie said.

Frank stared hard at him.

"Look, if you want, I'll come to your office tomorrow to talk, but not now. My little girl's sick. I just want to get her home. I don't know what the hell you want to talk to me about anyway. I don't know anything about any terrorists."

"Well, that's not exactly a true, is it Frankie? I mean, you do know *something* about terrorists, don't you?" Christie said.

"Not good to start a new relationship with a lie, Frank," Big Davie said from behind.

"I don't know what you're talking about." Frank sidestepped to get a better view of Samantha, and to get the big detective away from his back.

"No? Come on, Frankie, let's be honest with each other," Christie said. "You look a little nervous. And I sympathize, I really do. I mean, here we are, knowing everything about you, and you don't know me or Big Davie from Adam."

"Sammy!" Frank called to his daughter through the fence, but his mouth was dry and his voice stuck in his throat.

"Don't worry, Frank, she'll be fine. So, like I said, we know you, but you don't know us. How 'bout we play a game, huh? You show us yours, and we'll show you ours. And to prove we're good guys, we'll go first. Sound like fun, Frank?"

"I'm asking you nicely. *Please* get out of my way!"

"You've got a tone there, Frank. Didn't I already say to play nice?" Christie smirked as Big Davie laid Frank's shovel against a parking meter and stepped toward him.

"That's okay. I'll still show you ours," Christie continued. "We know you were a real big shot in Iraq. A war hero even—Purple Heart and everything. A top guy in EOD—Explosive Ordnance Detail, right?

"Explosive Ordnance *Disposal*," Frank corrected. "And that's all classified information."

"Yeah, right, whatever," Christie said, taking a notepad from his pocket and flipping it open. "Let's see," he continued. "You spent four months interrogating captured Taliban and Al Qaeda bomb makers in Afghanistan, Pakistan, and Iraq. Now, I gotta say, that qualifies you as knowing terrorists."

Christie wet his fingertips with his tongue and leafed through his notes. "Then there's a two-year tour in the Gulf pulling boom-boom pins out of hundreds of old mines that the towel-heads left lying around for our boys to step on. Oh sorry, Frank . . . the term *towel-head* offend you? Big Davie, I think I offended him."

"Maybe 'cause he married a towel-head and had a towel-head baby," Big Davie said.

"Oh, that's right, Sarah Mustaffa . . . got a picture of her right here. Not bad-looking, actually. Little Iraqi freedom fighter you hooked up with over there, eh, Frank?"

"She worked for Save the Children, she was an American citizen, and I suggest you watch your dirty mouth, you racist bastard," Frank said, taking a deep breath. For the second time that morning, he tried to use Samantha's relaxation trick, but it wasn't doing much good.

"Touchy, isn't he, Davie? Here's where we get to the sad part, and I must say, I'm real sorry to hear about what happened to the missus, Frank. An M16 can make an awful mess of someone. Terrible mistake, but I guess all towel-heads look the same over there. Must be tough . . . raising a sick kid all alone? Especially on such a tight budget."

"If you have a point to make, I suggest you make it now."

"I'm almost finished with my turn, Frank. Like I was saying, you marry little Miss Mustaffa, move to Jersey, and the Army loans you to the UN as some kind of a bomb expert-at-large. Says here you can take a nuke apart and put it back together blindfolded! That right, Frank? Some cojones on this one, eh, Big Davie? To wrap it up, your wife goes to Iraq to help the war orphans, gets shot accidentally by a U.S. soldier, and you get out of the Army and take over your dad's landscaping biz. That about sum it up, Frankie?"

"Yeah, that's real good—you've got my whole life in a file and actually know how to read. Now what the hell do you want?" Frank demanded, mentally measuring the distance between him and the two detectives.

"What we want is for you to answer some questions for us. First, why does an explosives expert who's pissed off at the U.S. Army for killing his wife go to work for Conrad Dinnick, a guy with access to weapons-grade germs? Second, why do you show up at this mosque every Friday, all buddy-buddy with a cleric who has ties to Islamic extremists? And third, why the hell have you stockpiled enough fertilizer in the past year to blow up Grand Central Station? Anything I'm missing, Davie?"

"As a matter of fact, yeah. Frankie, what were you doing at Roosevelt Island today when you weren't scheduled to be there—coincidentally a couple of hours before the mayor and governor are supposed to arrive, and just before a police boat mysteriously blows up?"

"You guys can't be serious," Frank croaked. "You think *I'm* a terrorist? I've spent five years straddling bombs for this country . . . they gave me the Medal of Honor, for Chrissakes!"

"Yeah, you're a real freakin' hero. Come on, you heard what we've got on you . . . you've got to admit it doesn't look good." Big Davie shook his head.

"Looks bad, Frank, real goddamn bad," Christie said. "But I promised you'd have a turn, and this is it. So go ahead, clear the air. If you've done nothing wrong, you've got nothing to worry about. Give us something to go with."

"I got nothing to give you, man. I don't know anything about a boat blowing up. I was on the island to make sure the job was done. The only fertilizer I have is on my lawn or in the back of my truck, and I've got nothing stockpiled. And the cleric here helps out with my daughter and—," Frank realized it didn't matter what he said. These guys were looking at him like he had TERRORIST tattooed across his forehead. They'd reached their verdict: guilty.

"If you think I'm a terrorist, why are you talking to me on the street? Why not just arrest me, label me an enemy combatant, lock me up, and throw away the key?"

"Oh jeez, Frankie, didn't I mention that?" asked Christie, his sardonic smile spreading across his face. "You *are* under arrest . . . we're just waiting for Social Services to get here and take away your kid."

Frank's heart pounded against his chest, and he could feel the oxygen squeezing out of his lungs, the way it had the first time he'd been in combat. He gulped for air.

"Social services . . . my daughter . . . please . . . she's sick, very, very sick . . . she can't be away from me . . . it will kill her . . . please . . ."

"You have the right to remain silent," Big Davie recited, reaching behind his back and producing a set of handcuffs. "Anything you say can, and will, be used against—"

As Big Davie grabbed his wrists, Frank dropped into a squatting position and then thrust upward with all his strength. The top of Frank's skull caught Big Davie under the jaw, and he heard the bones crack. Frank jabbed his left elbow into the detective's solar plexus, and the big man dropped to the cement.

Detective Christie was pulling his gun from his holster when Frank grabbed the shovel from against the meter and swung it in a sweeping arc. Its steel blade smashed against the side of Christie's head, knocking him face-first onto the sidewalk.

"Oh shit, oh shit, oh shit!" Frank cried out, dropping to his knees and collecting the guns and badges from the unconscious detectives.

"Daddy?"

Frank looked up into his daughter's pale, frightened face.

"Sammy, *get into the truck now!* Oh, honey, it's going to be okay. These are bad men . . . they were going to take you away from me."

A handful of women who had been praying were looking through the gate, pointing at Frank. He scooped up Samantha in his arms and stumbled to the truck.

"Why would they take me away? Why did you hurt them?"

Frank started the engine and pulled into traffic, trying to think straight . . . and trying to map out the fastest route to the Lincoln Tunnel.

He looked at his daughter, who was holding her prayer mat to her chest and staring at him, horrified.

"Don't look at me like that, Sammy. I'm not a monster. I'm not sure what just happened myself, but it's got something to do with me being in the Army and your mom being Iraqi . . . it's all so mixed up, I just can't explain it right now. Please believe me, I did what had to be done. And I promise, promise, promise that I'll make it right. Okay?"

Samantha began to weep.

CHAPTER 13

ZOE DUCKED BEHIND A HELIX-SHAPED FOUNTAIN as the hand-cuffed psychic and her three grim-faced companions crossed the atrium toward her. She snapped her palmtop shut and pulled out her earphone, dropping both into her bag. Crouching on the floor, she waited for the group to pass and plotted her next move.

She'd definitely recorded enough material for a block-buster news item and could envision the headline: PSYCHIC TERRORIST? RADIO READING PANICS CITY!

She also had a national scoop and potential Pulitzer Prize for reporting on BioWorld's secret Level 4 research lab in Hoboken.

She smiled, but then she had a realization: *This should be a slam dunk, but what do I tell the boss? Um . . . just FYI, I committed a felony by impersonating a government official. And, oh yeah, you know all those quotes? Obtained illegally while recording a private conversation.*

Zoe knew the editor would have two choice words for her: *You're fired.* Then he'd send another reporter out to scoop her on her own story.

No way will I let that happen. . . . Right now I gotta get a quick interview with Katherine to back it all up. I need her on the record. I'll research Hoboken later. I gotta follow them outside and get to her before they cart her off to police headquarters—or the loony bin.

Zoe peered around the fountain as Katherine walked past, looking as though she was being marched to the gallows. Zoe checked her watch to give the group a two-minute head start before tailing them to the front door. As she waited, Zoe saw something she'd never seen before: a perfect blue rose, the deep color of a sapphire. There were dozens of them, each one more beautiful than the next. She waited another minute, and then began moving through the foliage, jumping across a small stream and sliding across some mossy stones before emerging from the atrium forest and nearly running headlong into Conrad Dinnick. She took a few steps back and sat down on a small bench.

Conrad and the others had stopped in the front lobby. Katherine was staring at Daniel, but the three men were looking up at an enormous monitor suspended above the security desk. They were watching a live broadcast from the Roosevelt Island tram wheelhouse. The camera panned across the platform packed with city dignitaries and local celebrities, all jostling each other to be photographed with the mayor and governor.

A fidgety young reporter, identified at the bottom of the screen as a science specialist for New York First News, stared out mutely from the screen. Off camera, someone was loudly whispering, "You're up, you're up!" The reporter cleared his throat and launched into a nasal-voiced commentary:

"Good morning. We're coming to you live from the Roosevelt Island Tram as it launches into the future on what could ironically be a historic journey. In a minute or two, our camera crew will board the tram with the mayor, the governor, and the many distinguished guests you see behind me. We will then travel over the East River, reaching a height of 250 feet, before descending to the island to be on hand when BioWorld founder Conrad Dinnick officially opens his multibillion-dollar Supercomputer Re-Creation Center. Whoa . . . try saying that ten times fast!

"No, just joshing you, folks. What a treat it is to be here. This new Center is the most expensive single structure ever built in New York, and is home to the most advanced computer system in the

world—reportedly capable of sequencing genes hundreds of times faster than any other computer now in existence. Its potential for advancing genetic research is, well, mind-boggling.

"And I can't neglect to mention that the center will create hundreds of high-tech and biotech jobs right here in the heart of Manhattan—a big boost in these troubled times.

"So don't touch your remote, because right after the ribbon-cutting ceremony, Mr. Dinnick will be making a major announcement. No one knows the details, but we're told it has something to do with a process called 'genetic regeneration.' I can promise you that it will be big news. The last time Conrad Dinnick held a news conference, he announced that he'd isolated and 'turned off' the celleptic cancer gene . . . you'll recall he received his first Nobel Prize for that one. So stay tuned to New York First News, folks. Our exclusive coverage of this historic . . ."

A Dixieland band pushed through the crowd playing a peppy rendition of "When the Saints Go Marching In." The music drowned out the reporter, who, after trying to shout above the racket, shrugged and held his microphone toward a rail-thin banjo player who was singing:

> *We are trav'ling in the footsteps*
> *Of those who've gone before*
> *But we'll all be reunited,*
> *On a new and sunlit shore,*
>
> *Oh, when the saints go marching in,*
> *When the saints go marching in . . .*

"Well, there they go. I missed my ride," sighed Conrad, watching the mayor and governor wave from the TV screen and step onto the tram. Everyone else on the platform—the band, reporter, camera crew, and several police officers—climbed on board with them. The doors slid shut, and the tram jerked from the platform, crossing over Second Avenue. The reporter, who was inside the tram squeezing himself between the governor and mayor, went back on camera.

"Fasten your seat belts, folks. We're heading into the future, and it's going to be one heck of a ride," he said, as the tram climbed toward the top of the Queensboro Bridge.

Conrad turned away from the screen. "We'll take Ms. Haywood outside and let the police deal with her, and I'll take the company boat across to the island. Let's go," he commanded, motioning to Wilson and Daniel to follow.

"Daniel and I will monitor things here, sir, but first we'll escort you to the dock," Wilson said. "I'll have a boat pilot standing by, and you'll arrive on the island at the same time as the tram."

"Good."

As they passed the security desk, the guard who'd questioned Zoe earlier yelled after them, "Mr. Dinnick, Mr. Wilson, please use the side exit. We have—"

Conrad silenced the guard with a dismissive wave. "What we *don't* have is any more time to waste," he asserted, striding across the front lobby and out the revolving door.

On the street below, dozens of demonstrators were shoving against a line of police in riot gear. The crowd became frenzied when Katherine appeared above them, standing at the top of the Tower's marble staircase.

A wave of angry shouts rolled up the stairs as someone threw a bottle that shattered at Conrad's feet. Zoe stepped outside and was hit by a flying brick. It only grazed her cheek, but it sent a flood of adrenaline coursing through her body.

"We've got to get you out of here *now!*" Wilson shouted, releasing his hold on Katherine and grabbing Conrad by the arm. "Move back into the building. You can take the chopper across the river."

"Yes, the ch-ch-chopper . . . Dad, let's go back inside," Daniel said worriedly, taking Conrad's other arm.

"Do you see what you've done? *Do you see?!*" Conrad yelled at Katherine, as Wilson and Daniel pulled him backward toward the revolving door.

Katherine didn't hear him. She stood frozen, staring at the

sky in wild-eyed panic as the bright red Roosevelt Island tram glided above them and out over the East River.

Zoe ran toward Katherine, hoping to talk to her before the protesters reached them. She reached into her bag for her recorder.

"That's it!" Katherine screamed, looking at the tram. "That's it . . . *that's it* . . . that's the ski lift I saw . . . we have to stop it . . . it's going to . . . someone stop it before it . . . it's going to—"

A man halfway down the stairs, wearing a leather jacket and a Captain America helmet, was glaring at Katherine. "Hey, psychic! I see someone already cuffed you. I guess I'm too late to make you my last collar!" he yelled. "How dare you talk about my son . . . they handed out those medals for bravery and sacrifice—not for phony psychics to exploit!" He opened his jacket and began pulling something out of his pants pocket.

But all Zoe saw was the butt of a gun sticking out of the man's leather coat, and his hand moving toward it. Instead of her recorder, Zoe pulled the latest-model stun gun from her reporter's knapsack, jerked her arm up, and squeezed the trigger. Two darts hit the man's chest, pierced his skin, and pumped enough electricity into him to completely disrupt his nervous system. His gun fell out of his jacket and clattered down the steps. He collapsed, convulsing violently until Zoe released the trigger. She looked at him, then back at Katherine, making eye contact with the psychic for the first time.

"I'm too late. . . ." Katherine said, looking up at the tram.

Zoe opened her mouth to ask her what she meant, but didn't get the chance. The blast hit her like a sledgehammer, lifting her off her feet and slamming her against the Tower wall. She dropped to the ground and rolled onto her side, with the wind knocked out of her and her stomach muscles contracting violently as she tried to breathe. She was beginning to black out when the air finally filled her lungs in a hot, acrid rush. She gagged, coughing until she thought her ribs would crack. Her eyes burned with ash and smoke, and she rubbed them hard until she could see.

Everyone who'd been near her—the police, the demonstrators, Conrad and his son, Wilson, and Katherine—had been knocked down. Zoe looked toward the river. The center tower of the Queensboro Bridge was listing to the northeast like the topmast of a sinking ship. A great, yawning groan of stretching steel filled her ears, ending with an abrupt snap. She stared in disbelief as hundreds of people leapt from their cars onto the swaying bridge and ran for their lives.

The bridge seemed to moan in pain for several minutes before its upper roadway collapsed onto the lower level, crushing hundreds of cars. The whole structure shuddered, and a long section dropped into the East River, creating huge waves. Several abandoned cars teetered on the edges of the severed bridge before slipping over and dropping into the water below. Dozens of vehicles bobbed downstream, spinning around in the current once or twice before sinking beneath the surface. Except for the terrified neighing of a few police horses, there was a moment of stunned silence.

Then the screaming began.

The bridge's wounded tower screeched as it twisted around, snagging and breaking the steel cable supporting the tram. The wire whistled as it snaked though the air, and the tram plunged toward the water more than a hundred feet below, disappearing in the thick cloud of smoke now blowing across the river.

Zoe looked over at Conrad, who'd gotten to his feet just in time to see the bridge's pillar break away from its moorings and slice his Re-Creation Center like the blade of a giant guillotine. A series of explosions ripped through the length of the building, culminating in an enormous blast that sent entire sections of steel wall sailing off both sides of the island. A fireball shot up, leaving a thick, dark cloud hanging in the air.

Conrad stared at the crumbled, fiery ruins of the Re-Creation Center. Burning ash landed on his sleeve, and he ripped off the smoldering jacket, tossing it to the ground. From the top of the BioWorld Tower steps, he had a panoramic view of the devastation. Fire was everywhere.

"Oh my God, oh my God. My Center . . . and all those people," he moaned, dropping to his knees and burying his face in his hands.

Some of Conrad's security detail rushed to his side.

"Grab that psychic!" Conrad ordered. "Find out what's going on. How did she know? Find out if this attack was directed at me."

Then he suddenly looked up, turned westward, and gasped.

"We have to stop them," said Conrad, jumping to his feet. "Whoever did this—if they get to the lab in New Jersey, they could kill us all. We have to get to Hoboken!"

CHAPTER 14

THE DODGE JERKED FORWARD, and Frank thought he'd been rear-ended until he heard the explosion—a boom so powerful that it shook the buildings along Lexington Avenue.

"Daddy?" Samantha asked, clutching his arm. "What is it? Did a plane crash?"

"Jesus."

"Daddy . . . is it a plane crash?"

"No, no honey, it's not a plane. It sounded like a bomb, a big one. But it's a long way from here, so don't worry," Frank said, flooring the gas pedal and screeching down the street.

He sped through traffic like the truck had a force field he was sure other vehicles couldn't penetrate, cutting off two taxis and a dump truck to get into the buses-only lane.

It was a risky move. Driving in the restricted lane increased his chances of being pulled over, but he had no choice. He had to get to the tunnel before the cops he'd knocked out at the mosque came to and reported him.

If they ever come to, Frank thought. *I hit them both so hard that I probably killed them . . . but don't think about that. Focus, Frank, focus.* He pounded his fist against the steering wheel when the bus he was following stopped to pick up a long line of passengers.

Frank looked over at Samantha. Her eyes were closed, and

sweat dripped from her forehead. Her face was ashen and her lips were trembling. He brushed his fingers across her arm, felt the coldness of her skin, and panicked.

"Sammy? Sammy?" He shook her roughly. "Wake up honey! Please wake up!"

"I *am* awake, Franklin."

"How you feelin'?"

"About you beating up two policemen? Not good."

"Well, no, not that. I mean, how are you *feeling* feeling? You're sweating, but you're cold. Your lips were trembling."

"I feel a little sick, but I think it's because of your driving. I'll be okay when we're home."

"We'll be home soon."

"And my lips weren't trembling; I was praying."

"Jesus, honey, you just finished praying at the mosque."

"Yeah, well, that was before you hit those guys. That'll take *lots* of praying to square with You-Know-Who."

"Sammy, you know I don't believe in hurting people."

"You've got a funny way of showing it."

Frank pressed down on the truck's horn and held it for a good 30 seconds. *Move it, move it, move it.* The bus driver stuck a hand out his window and pointed his middle finger upward at Frank.

"Damn it, Sammy! Those guys were assholes. I mean *really bad* guys! They would've taken you away and stuck you in a foster home. Just because they've got badges, Sam, doesn't mean . . . look, they're exactly like the ignorant jarheads who killed your mom for being a Muslim and—"

"I heard what they said. I know what they think. I know you're scared for me. But you shouldn't have hit them."

"Sammy, you've *memorized* the friggin' Bible, right? What about 'an eye for an eye'?"

Samantha sighed. "Exodus 21:23 . . . *life for life, eye for eye, tooth for tooth* . . . that sort of thing?"

Frank nodded, "Yeah, exactly. See?"

"No one poked out your eye, Frank. And Jesus revised Exodus

in Matthew 5:39: '. . . *whosoever shall smite thee on thy right cheek, turn to him the other also.*' You didn't do much cheek turning back there, did you, Frank?"

Frank checked the rearview mirror. Traffic was bumper-to-bumper as far as he could see, but there was a flashing red light about 20 blocks back, moving slowly through the gridlock toward them.

"Okay, okay. Sammy. Let's skip the Bible lesson. I hit them, and I shouldn't have. I hope they're okay. Is that why you're praying, so they'll get better?"

"No, I was praying we get the hell out of here before you get arrested. So *please,* Frank, if we're heading for the Lincoln Tunnel, get off Lex, cut through Central Park, and then head south."

"Okay, Sam, jeeze," Frank laughed. "Better make up your mind what you're going to be when you grow up: a preacher, a shrink, or a taxi driver because you—," Frank stopped in mid-sentence and bit his tongue.

"It's okay," Samantha said quietly. "You can say, 'When you grow up.' I'm going to, you know, and I'm going to be all those things. . . . I just have to wait until my next life, that's all."

Frank turned right on to 72nd Street, reaching out to touch Samantha again. She was a little warmer. Sometimes that's how it was for her after chemo: shivering one minute, warm the next.

I've got to get her somewhere safe, get her to bed, he fretted.

They stopped for a red light at Madison Avenue, and he checked the rearview mirror again. No sign of the cops. Leaning over, he kissed his daughter's cheek.

"Listen, kid, I've screwed things up royally, and I've got to make them right. So, instead of going home, I'm taking you to your Aunt Lucy's in Connecticut for a couple days, and she'll drive you up to your Aunt Lorna's in Toronto, okay?"

"What? Go to *Canada?* Why can't we just go home?"

"Because the police know where we live, and they'll find us at Lucy's soon enough. If you stay here, they'll try to put you in a foster home, and that's not going to happen."

"But, Daddy—"

"It's going to be okay. I'll come up to visit you next weekend. I just have to straighten things out with the police, and
then we'll be together."

"Swear, Daddy, swear you're telling the truth."

"I swear it."

"Swear on Mommy's grave."

"Sam . . . I—"

They heard another explosion, much smaller than the first.

They both turned, looking through the rear window at the
giant plume of smoke rising up behind them, somewhere near
the East River.

"Daddy?" Samantha clutched his arm. "What's happening? Is it another bomb?!"

"No, Sammy, don't worry about bombs. Someone's probably just setting off some fireworks."

"But you said it was a bomb, Daddy!"

"Forget what I said."

Frank floored it, screeching across Madison Avenue toward
Central Park.

CHAPTER 15

JACK OPENED HIS EYES. His ears buzzed, and his mouth tasted of burnt toast. He tried to move, but couldn't, so he lay still, staring into the fading sunlight.

He didn't have a clue where he was, but recognized the nasty lump of remorse churning in the pit of his stomach. It was the same sickening feeling he used to get every Monday morning after waking from a bender. No memory of the weekend, just a gnawing sense that he'd done something ugly and would pay for it later.

I haven't touched a drink in years . . . right? He tried to remember, realizing that he didn't know where or *when* he was. He closed his eyes. Fragments of memory began banging against each other: Susan's face, a carriage ride, a gunshot, his motorcycle, a bridge, a gun, that voice . . . the same voice that was calling to him now.

"It's not your time just yet—hang on, you'll be okay."

Jack opened his eyes. Someone, a woman he thought, was hovering over him, her face hidden in shadow, as a dark cloud began to swallow the sun.

"Susan?" he whispered.

"No, but Susan's here with us," she said softly.

Jack recognized the voice but couldn't place it.

"Your name's Jack, right? Yes, Jack. We don't have much

time, so listen closely. Susan has a message for you that I'm trying to understand . . . something happened, something horrible. Whatever it was, she needs you to know that it wasn't
your fault. She passed so you'd be here today. You have to finish something. I don't know what this is, but she's saying, *'Follow the story.'* Now she's . . . I'm sure of it . . . she's showing me
a baby, in the arms of St. Thomas. To me that means that she
wants you to forgive yourself for something and start living
again. And Jack, she also says, *'Tomorrow will be a better day.'* Do
you understand this? *'Tomorrow will be a better day.'* Do you
under—"

The woman's face vanished, and her last sentence was
drowned out by a commanding male voice shouting, "On your
feet, psychic, you're coming with us!"

Psychic? Jack thought, the events of the day breaking
through his delirium. *Oh God, what did I do? Why didn't I just kill
myself . . . I must be—*

"Crazy Jack Morgan! It is you, isn't it? I knew I recognized
that helmet. What in the hell are *you* doing here?"

Another female face was looking down at him. But the sun
was now completely engulfed by clouds, so he could easily
make out her features. *She's beautiful,* Jack realized, staring into
her eyes—the soft green color of old Coke bottles.

"Who are you? Where am I?"

"My name is Zoe Crane. You'd better relax for a minute. I
zapped you with my stun gun when you went for your pistol.
You should be fine in a couple minutes, but if you mess with
me, I'll stun you again."

"I can hardly breathe, lady. I'm not going to be messing with
anybody."

Zoe looked at him warily, then cradled his head in the
crook of her arm and held a bottle of water she'd fished out from
her knapsack to his lips. As Jack gulped down the water, Zoe
looked at the handsome face encased in the ridiculous helmet—the same one he'd worn in the photo accompanying a
story she'd read about him in *The Trumpet* archives. *Poor guy sees*

his wife get whacked right in front of him . . . but why the hell does he go postal a decade later? And why today of all days? There must be a scoop here somewhere.

She took the bottle away from his lips and gently wiped the soot and ash from his eyelids.

"Feel better?" she asked.

"All pins and needles."

"Good, the shock's wearing off. Let's get you up."

She slipped her arm around his shoulders and pulled him until he was sitting up, facing the river.

The breeze off the water burned Jack's face. He rubbed his eyes, and then he rubbed them again. He stared at the dozens of people at the bottom of the steps: Some were coughing, others were calling for help, and many more were being tended to by police officers.

He looked up at the Queensboro Bridge, shrouded in smoke billowing from a huge fire in the center of Roosevelt Island. As the smoke cleared for a second, Jack saw the gaping hole in the bridge's crippled frame. Struggling to catch his breath, he gasped, "Holy Mary Mother of God, what's happened? What the hell has happened?"

"I don't know," Zoe replied. "I guess it was an explosion."

"Again. They did it again, didn't they? Another attack? Those goddamned, murderous bastards!" Jack shouted, then turned to Zoe. "How many . . . how many did they kill this time?"

"I don't know. I saw people running off the bridge and people running on the island . . . I just don't know. But what the hell do you care? You showed up here with a gun trying to kill people yourself!"

"What are you talking about? I didn't try to kill anyone."

"You were pulling a gun out of your jacket. You were going to shoot the psychic, Jack. I saw you, and I heard you. I *stopped* you, for Christ's sake!"

"I wasn't going to shoot her. I was just going to show her something that belonged to my boy and tell her to stop exploiting people's sorrow. I wasn't going to kill *her*. Not that it's any of your business, but I was going to kill *myself* today. I'd already be dead if I hadn't heard that psychic on the radio."

"That's pure bullshit. Going to kill *yourself?* Yeah, like I'm going to buy that line, especially from Crazy Jack Morgan."

"Look for yourself. There's only one round in the cylinder, and that bullet has my name on it. I just wanted to scare her. I would never shoot an unarmed woman."

"What, are you a chauvinist, too?"

Jack grabbed Zoe by the arm, pulling her toward him until their eyes were just inches apart.

"Who *are* you?" he demanded.

"I told you—Zoe Crane. I'm a reporter." She hesitated. "For *The Trumpet.*"

"*The Trumpet?* Oh, that's just perfect!" He turned his back to her and stared at the growing fire across the river. "Got yourself a nice little story, don't you?"

Zoe picked up Jack's gun and opened the cylinder. *Like he said, just one round in here.* She shook the bullet into her palm. *Jesus, he literally meant that it had his name on it.* She read the words etched on the casing of the bullet: *Jack Morgan: Guilty of uxoricide.* Zoe had read enough autopsy reports to know that *uxoricide* meant murdering your wife.

Zoe slipped the bullet back, closed the cylinder, and handed the gun back to Jack.

"It's your gun, and it's your life, so do what you want with them. You said the psychic was a liar. Maybe . . . that's pretty much what I've always thought, too. But that woman predicted that this would happen today, and she predicted there'd be more explosions. I don't know what Katherine Haywood ever did to you, or why you want to kill yourself, but take a look out there," she said, pointing to the ruined bridge and wounded people. "If anything like *that* is going to happen again today, I need to find out where and when. So I need you to tell me what she said to you," Zoe said.

"What do you mean, what she said to me?"

"When you were lying here. She was leaning over you, talking to you. What did she say?"

"That was *her?* I thought I was hallucinating."

"You weren't. Did she say where the other bombs might be?"

"What? No, she . . . she said . . ."

Suddenly Jack remembered: *She said that tomorrow would be a better day . . . the same thing Susan said to me every morning. How could she have known?* Jack wondered, incredulous.

"Well? Are you going to tell me?" Zoe insisted.

"I can't remember," Jack said, thinking he really must have been hallucinating.

"No comment, huh? Well, I'm a reporter, and right now she's the only story in the world, so I'm following her."

"What?" Jack said.

"Katherine seemed to know exactly what was about to happen. She knew about the explosions and the tram, so I'm going to follow the story. Maybe I can write something that matters for a change."

"Wait! She said that to me. She said, 'Follow the story.'"

Jack and Zoe stared at each other. There were wailing sirens coming from the street and helicopters swarming overhead.

"Tell me something. Are you still a cop?"

"Technically, yeah, until the end of the day."

"Really? You've got a shield?"

"Yeah."

"Good. I think Katherine is going to Hoboken; I overheard her saying it. But by now the tunnels will be closed to civilians because of what's happened here. Will you help me get across the river?"

Jack looked at the burning island and collapsed bridge. "Yeah, I'll help you," he said at last, "and I'll make her my last arrest. But I don't know if I can get to my bike—it's hard for me to move. "

Zoe lifted Jack's arm across her shoulder and hoisted him up. She helped him down the stairs, through the mounting frenzy on the street, to the curb where his battered Harley lay in the gutter.

"I don't have the strength to lift it," Jack told her.

"Don't worry—six years of sparring might finally pay off," Zoe replied, grabbing a long handlebar and the frame just beneath the seat, then pulling the bike upright.

Jack eased onto the seat, kick-started the bike with relatively little effort, and took off his helmet and passed it to Zoe. As she climbed on the seat behind him, he said, "Wear the helmet and tell me which way to go."

"The tunnel. Take the Lincoln Tunnel."

CHAPTER 16

CONRAD STOOD ON THE EASTERN EDGE of the BioWorld Tower roof, staring down at the fire raging on Roosevelt Island. A menacing cloud was forming over the island, and the orange and blue flames shimmered savagely in the spreading darkness.

The blades of the BioWorld helicopter were slicing the air in a high-pitched whine when Wilson approached Conrad. "The bird's ready to fly, sir. Time to board."

Conrad walked toward the helicopter. Wilson held Katherine's cuffed wrists; Daniel crouched by the cockpit door talking to the pilot; and a half-dozen guards stood around the chopper, rifles at the ready.

Katherine leaned over, pressing her mouth against Conrad's ear so he'd hear her over the spinning blades.

"Don't get in that helicopter—it's dangerous. I need to talk to you alone, *now*," she said.

Wilson immediately yanked Katherine from Conrad and dragged her to the helicopter as she screamed, "No, no, no! Dear God, don't put me in there. I'm not getting into that death trap! Let go of me! *Get your stinking paws off me!*"

She twisted around and kneed Wilson in the groin. He doubled over, and she made a run for it, straight into an armed guard standing at the roof's only door.

I'm 120 stories up—where in heaven's name am I going to go?

she thought desperately, spinning to make a last-minute appeal to Conrad.

"Please . . . this helicopter . . . it's not safe!"

Wilson had recovered and was heading straight for her.

"Conrad, believe me, this man is not acting in your best interests . . . or mine. He's dangerous."

Wilson grabbed her, slapped his hand over his mouth, dragged her to the helicopter, and threw her in. A guard was already sitting in the passenger cabin, and Wilson told him: "Keep her quiet. Do you understand what your other orders are?"

"Yes, sir," the guard said, looking across the roof at Conrad.

"Wilson, that Haywood woman is in hysterics," Conrad said with concern. "Are you sure this helicopter's safe?"

"Absolutely, sir."

"Even with the solar storm?"

"No problem, sir," Wilson assured his boss, starting to climb into the passenger cabin.

Conrad caught him by the sleeve.

"Wait, Wilson. I don't want you to come with us," Conrad said.

"Excuse me, sir? The city and BioWorld may be under attack. I'm not leaving your side. Besides, Hoboken is a prime target."

"Don't you think I know that? I need you to contact Washington and the New York National Guard. We need to at least *triple* our security presence at all our facilities—especially the Level 4 lab in Hoboken!" Conrad ordered.

"Of course, sir, I'm on it already—I guarantee I'll take care of it personally. As far as security is concerned, you have nothing to worry about."

"Then I don't need you in Hoboken. I need you here to protect my son, and to protect our headquarters. Guard the building at all costs—my life's work is in here. I want you to seal the Tower tight and start up our oxygen-production units. If anything goes wrong in Hoboken, the Tower is the safest place to be."

"Sir, I don't—"

"That's an order, understood?"

"Yes, sir, if you insist."

"Fine. And take the cuffs off Miss Haywood."

"Unadvisable, sir."

"She seems ready to talk, but might not be so forthcoming if we still have her chained up."

Wilson reluctantly gave an order to a guard inside the helicopter, and he unlocked Katherine's cuffs.

"Let me out of here! Let me out of here!" she began screaming again, banging on the window.

The guard restrained Katherine, pressing his thumb and forefinger against her throat, and in a few moments, her head dropped forward.

"What have you done?" Conrad yelled.

"Relax, sir," Wilson assured him. "Our man just performed a standard Army hold used to subdue unruly prisoners. He simply stopped her oxygen supply for a few seconds to put her to sleep. She'll be awake and screaming before you get to Hoboken."

"I'm starting to wonder about your tactics, Wilson."

"Just doing my job, sir. And don't worry, your son is safe with me," Wilson said, saluting and walking over to the pilot's window to issue some final orders.

Conrad approached Daniel and wrapped his arms around him. It was the first time he remembered hugging his son since he was a child. He hated to admit it, but he knew he'd always favored Michael. And after Michael had gotten sick, then committed suicide, he took much of his anger out on his surviving son.

"Danny, I've said some terrible things to you today, and over the last . . . well, I mean, I've never really been a good father to you. This morning's ceremony was to have been dedicated in Michael's memory . . . Project PAT . . . all his work . . . and now . . . and now—"

"Don't . . . wor-wor-worry about it," Daniel said, breaking the embrace abruptly.

"I'll make it all up to you, Danny. I have so much to make up for." Conrad began climbing into the helicopter, but turned back to face his son. "I, uh . . . I love you, Danny. If anything happens to me, BioWorld is yours. Finish Project PAT."

Conrad slid the cabin door shut and sat down beside Katherine.

"You can count on it!" Daniel yelled from the roof as the helicopter lifted off.

Wilson walked over to Daniel and put his arm around his shoulders, saying, "Don't worry . . . it's all for the best."

Conrad fastened his safety belt and leaned over to clasp the belt of the still-unconscious Katherine.

"Are you're sure she's all right?" Conrad asked the guard.

"She's fine, sir."

The helicopter lifted off the roof, swung out over the East River, U-turned toward Hoboken, and began flying over Midtown.

Katherine woke with a start, looked out the window, and saw scores of flashing red lights hundreds of feet below.

"Oh God . . . how could you have let them put us in here? I told you this was dangerous. You'll get us both killed," Katherine whispered frantically to Conrad.

"Calm down, you're fine. And we'll be perfectly safe, Ms. Haywood . . . we'll land in Hoboken in five minutes. What happened to the bridge and on the island will be nothing, *nothing,* compared to what could happen if someone attacks the other lab. Now, you said you wanted to talk to me. If you do, you'd better start now. What you said on the radio this morning about the explosions . . . I want to know how you knew about them."

Katherine looked at the guard, then back at Conrad.

"Put on your headset, would you?" Conrad asked the man.

As soon as the guard's ears were covered, Katherine began talking urgently.

"First of all, we're in real danger. We should never have gotten on this helicopter, and—and—there's so much coming through to me. Wait, let me focus . . . I have an older female coming through to me . . . like a mom . . . and her son or grandson . . . wait, wait . . . they want you to trust me . . . look, I may have predicted what happened at the bridge, but I had nothing to do with it. Do you believe me?"

"Believe *what?* That spirits confided in you about a bomb plot?" Conrad was incredulous. "I don't believe in spirits or an afterlife. Maybe you've been hypnotized or have some form of extrasensory perception . . . so if you sense something about Hoboken, I'm all ears and willing to listen. But don't expect me to believe in spirits. I already told you, I'm a man of science."

Katherine put her hand on Conrad's. "How do you think I knew about your mother and the blue roses?"

Conrad sighed, "Newspapers, magazines, television—take your pick."

"Then how can I know that when you were a boy your mother told you that you could play God?"

"Radio, Internet, chat groups, private detectives . . ."

"And how," Katherine squeezed his hand tightly, her voice filled with alarm, "do I know that you murdered your mother?"

Conrad didn't have time to respond. In one swoop, the guard sitting across from them lunged at Conrad, unfastened his seat belt, and slid open the passenger cabin door.

"Sorry, sir, this is where you get out."

"Are you crazy?!" Conrad yelled at the man, kicking him with both his feet.

Katherine screamed. The helicopter suddenly rolled to one side, and the guard, reeling from Conrad's blow, stumbled backward and out the door.

Katherine held on to Conrad's arm, preventing him from falling out as well. They could both see the guard tumbling through the air until he smashed into the roof of St. Patrick's Cathedral.

"What did I tell you!" Katherine shouted, and then immediately began centering herself. She closed her eyes and concentrated on channeling positive energy, visualizing the two of them emerging safely from the helicopter.

Conrad closed the door and pounded on the glass wall separating the passenger cabin from the pilot.

"What the hell is going on?!"

"A solar storm is frying my instrument panel . . . hold on, I've got to try to put this thing down!" the pilot responded, his voice barely audible through the glass.

The BioWorld helicopter dropped suddenly, falling hundreds of feet in seconds. Conrad saw the crowded square of Rockefeller Center hurtling toward him, and he turned to Katherine and said, "I'm sorry."

Katherine began pounding her fist against Conrad's chest.

"Why didn't you listen to me? I told you, I warned you that this would happen."

"I know, I know," Conrad groaned, wrapping his arms around her tightly.

The helicopter pulled up just above the ground, passed over the center's concourse, banked hard to the left, and headed north up Fifth Avenue. They were flying so close to the ground that Conrad could see the faces of startled tourists videotaping them from the open upper level of a double-decker bus.

They shot up Fifth, passing between The Plaza Hotel and Trump Tower, and crossed into Central Park, clipping treetops along the way.

Katherine and Conrad clung to each other as the helicopter began spiraling downward. As the ground rushed up, Conrad's mind went blank except for a single memory: the day he brought his sons to Central Park on their eighth birthday, a crisp December afternoon. His gift to them was to be their first skating lesson, but as soon as they'd arrived at the rink, he was called away to the lab. A nanny taught them to skate.

The helicopter plunged into a clump of trees, and everything went dark.

CHAPTER 17

FRANK BARRELED ACROSS FIFTH AVENUE and entered Central Park at 72nd, realizing too late that the park was closed to vehicles at that hour. He smashed through a groundskeeper's wooden traffic barricade, which bounced over his hood, cracking his windshield. The road forked immediately, and he made a fast left to head southbound toward the tunnel.

"Daddy, *look out!*" Samantha shouted.

A young mother was pushing a stroller across the road directly in front of them. Frank cranked the steering wheel so hard that the truck's right wheels left the ground, nearly flipping the pickup onto its side. The tires screeched as the truck hit the pavement again, fishtailing downhill in the wrong direction.

"Damn it, I missed the turn! I'm going north!" Frank shouted, honking at a throng of pedestrians gawking at the dark cloud of smoke rising over the Upper East Side. "You okay, Sammy?" he asked his daughter

"Please—please, please, *please,* slow down, Daddy. You're going to kill someone. You're really scaring me."

"I'm sorry, sweetie, but we've got no time. I won't hit anyone, I promise." He glanced at his daughter and forced a smile. "Hey, people are easy to miss. You should try driving through a minefield with tank gunners shooting at you. At least no one's shooting at *us,* huh?" Frank said nervously, trying to laugh.

"No, but they will if you don't *slow down.* You're not even supposed to be driving in the park. The police are probably looking for us everywhere and—"

"Don't worry *too* much about the police, Sammy. They've got lots of other things to worry about at the moment."

She sat silently for a minute, then looked sternly at her father.

"I want you to tell me something, Frank, and tell me the truth."

"Anything, Sammy."

"How'd you know it wasn't a plane crash we just heard?"

"How did I—," Frank swerved again, this time narrowly avoiding a pack of cyclists.

Jesus, don't these people even know what the hell is going on? He stuck his head out the window and yelled back at them, "The goddamned city is blowing up, for Christ's sake!"

As they passed behind the Metropolitan Museum of Art, he said, "I know I just said not to worry *too* much about cops, but we've got to worry a little. They could be coming up behind us, so I can't turn around. So hang on, kid—I'm going to detour."

He veered left, jumping the curb and ending up on the bridle path. A half-dozen horses bolted with their riders as Frank pulled a U-turn in front of them, heading up a steep embankment and onto the jogging track circling the Central Park reservoir.

"All right, okay. We're halfway home, Sammy," he said, gunning the engine and racing westward around the southern end of the track.

"Stop, Daddy, *stop!* I'm going to be sick. . . ."

Frank pulled off the path, parking in the shade of a tall maple tree.

"What is it?" he asked, unfastening her seat belt and taking her into his arms. "I'm so sorry, honey . . . but I've just got to get you out of here before it's too late."

Samantha pressed her head against his chest. She was cold and shivering. Her breathing was shallow, and she was wheezing.

"Okay, I guess we can stop for a minute. We'll take a little breather, and you'll feel better. Okay, honey? You just need some air."

Samantha rarely let Frank carry her, but for the second time today, he cradled her in his arms, and his heart broke at how thin she'd become. Samantha closed her eyes for a moment. When she opened them, she saw her mother standing on a sunny patch of grass just a few feet away. Her eyes closed again.

Frank carried her from the truck, took a bottle of water from the cooler in back, and set her down gently on a bench overlooking the reservoir. A small bronze plaque affixed to the backrest was engraved, *In loving memory of Maria Christoff.*

"This is a pretty spot, Daddy. When you get paid for the Roosevelt Island job, will you buy me a memorial bench here?"

"Don't start, Sammy. You'll be buying *me* a memorial bench. And don't forget, you promised to dance with me at your wedding." Frank looked at his watch and softly pinched Samantha's small wrist between his fingers, hoping to discreetly gauge her pulse.

"It's very weak today, isn't it," she said faintly, and then turned and vomited on the grass. "I'm sorry, Daddy. I wish—"

"Why are *you* sorry?" Frank held her close, wiped her face, and kissed her forehead. "I'm the one who's made you sick with my crazy driving." He gave her a sip of water to rinse her mouth.

"No, the cancer made me sick. Your driving always makes me puke," Samantha laughed weakly.

"Oh, honey . . . you're so cold."

"I'm scared."

"I know you are, but we gotta get out of here now. You'll feel better at your aunt's. It's safe there."

"I'm not scared for me. I'm scared for you . . . and for everybody else in the city. Daddy?"

"Yeah, Sammy?"

"Pray with me?"

Frank stroked his daughter's neck tenderly, resting his fingers on her throat and counting her heartbeats. Her pulse *was* weak, but at least it was steady. He rubbed the back of her neck, and she began to feel warmer.

"Please pray with me."

"You know that's the only thing I can't do for you, sweetie. Please don't ask me to."

"Daddy, you have to stop blaming God for what happened to Mommy, and for what's going to happen to me."

Frank was silent for a moment. Finally, he said, "If I did believe in God, I'd have to hate Him for taking your mother from us, and that's something I can't do. So I don't believe in Him, Sammy. Not anymore. Let's drop it, okay?"

"How many times do I have to tell you, Dad," Samantha reminded him with a fragile smile, "God's a *woman*."

"Oh yeah, I forgot," Frank laughed. "Then, I don't believe in *Her*. Honey, we've really got to go now."

"Wait."

"What is it?"

"How did you know it was a bomb, Frank?"

"You know my Army job was doing bomb stuff, remember? To this day, I still recognize the sounds of those things."

Frank stood up with Samantha in his arms. She rested her head on his shoulder, and whispered, "Wait."

"Now what?"

"If you don't believe in God . . . if you don't ever pray again . . . how will you hear me talk to you when I'm gone?"

Frank walked silently to the truck, trying not to let Samantha see his face as he gently placed her on the seat and leaned over to fasten her seat belt.

That's when he heard it.

A thick stand of pine trees blocked his view, but he knew the sound. It was a chopper in distress.

What the hell? Can't be, not here. Is this some kind of flashback?

Am I going nuts? Frank thought. But then suddenly, it was above them, maybe a hundred yards away—a private helicopter struggling to stay up, but quickly heading down.

The pine trees in front of him began snapping like dried wishbones as the battered fuselage of the chopper plowed through the grove. It burst from the tree line, skipped across a patch of lawn like a stone skimming across a still lake, and slammed into an old oak tree less than 20 feet from Frank's truck.

Frank jumped into the cab and reached for the ignition. "The keys! Where are the freakin' keys?"

"Go help them!"

"Sammy, the goddamn gas . . . give me the keys, I've to get you out of here. *Give them to me!*"

"Go help them, Frank!"

Frank jumped from the truck, choking on the spreading fumes, and splashed through a puddle of leaking fuel toward the downed chopper.

He saw the pilot's grotesquely twisted head sticking through the shattered windshield and knew instantly that he was dead. The cabin door was open, so Frank pulled out the first body he saw: a man with a blood-covered face. Frank plucked a shard of glass from the man's temple, wiped his eyes with his sleeve, and turned him in the direction of the Dodge.

"Can you walk?" Frank asked.

"I think so."

"Good. Then *run* to that truck."

As the man moved toward the truck, he yelled back to Frank, pointing into the chopper's cabin. But Frank couldn't hear a word the man was saying—his voice was completely drowned out by a familiar, angry thrum that sent a shiver down his spine.

Frank looked up. Hovering just above him was a U.S. Army Apache attack helicopter, its two 30mm machine-gun cannons pointed directly at him, and its 16 Hellfire missiles fastened to its underbelly, ready to launch.

My God, this is becoming a freakin' war zone! Did the Army just shoot this chopper out of the sky!? Frank wondered.

The Apache suddenly pulled up and away from him, banking low and to the east until it was out of sight.

Frank stepped into the cabin of the downed chopper. A red-haired woman was slumped over, tangled in her safety belt. He put his hand on her chest and pushed down hard, trying to slip the shoulder strap around her. She opened her eyes, looked at his hand, smacked him hard across the face, and passed out again. Frank managed to pull the woman through the straps, hoisted her long body over his shoulders in a firefighter's carry position, and sprinted back to the pickup.

The bleeding man was sitting in the back, so Frank let the woman's body slide from his shoulders onto the man's lap.

"I'll pay you $100,000 to take us to Hoboken," the man said.

"Buddy, you'll be lucky if I can get you ten feet before that thing blows," Frank said, jumping into the cab and sticking out his hand to Samantha.

"Keys!"

"I put them in the ignition."

Seconds later they were zigzagging across the park's Great Lawn. Frank looked into his rearview mirror and watched the flames of the exploding helicopter shoot into the sky. Then he looked at his daughter.

He could see her lips moving, but he could barely hear what she was saying. She was whispering so softly: "Okay, Mommy . . . I will . . . I promise . . . don't worry."

CHAPTER 18

THE LIMOUSINE IDLED 30 FEET BELOW THE STREETS OF MANHATTAN as the driver waited in darkness for the massive garage door to open.

This door of the BioWorld Tower was known in engineering circles as the strongest ever manufactured—a massively thick gate of solid tungsten that was capable of withstanding a direct hit from high-powered explosives.

A series of heavy metallic cracks echoed as the door's bolts retracted, followed by a steady hissing as the Tower's air lock was broken. The door rolled up like a two-ton Venetian blind.

As soon as there was enough clearance, the dark limo emerged from the basement, heading up the ramp toward York Avenue.

But before it reached the street, a dozen NYPD Operation Atlas officers had the car surrounded. They all wore gas masks and bulletproof vests and had their weapons trained on the long, dark car.

"Stop or we'll shoot!" shouted one of the officers. His order was muted, muffled by the thick gas mask, but his intent was clear.

The limo halted immediately, and as the tinted rear passenger window rolled down, a hand emerged and presented a BioWorld Security DNA/Photo ID, and a security pass issued by the Department of Homeland Security.

The lead officer approached with his shotgun leveled at the window, leaned forward, and inspected the credentials.

"John Wilson, BioWorld Security Chief," Wilson said, from inside the car.

"General John Wilson? Boy am I glad it's you in there, sir. I wish circumstances were different. Damn city's blowing up around us, and—"

"Do I know you?"

"Sir, yes, sir. Sergeant Peter Crighton—um, well, you knew me when I was *Captain* Crighton, sir. It was my honor to serve under you in Desert Storm," the sergeant said, slipping his gas mask up off his face so it sat on his head like a baseball cap.

"Your weapon is in my face. Please lower it."

"Sorry, sir," Crighton said, pointing his shotgun at the ground and signaling his men to do the same.

"That's better. Of course I remember you. Fightin' Crighton—the man who single-handedly took out three Iraqi tanks in ten minutes. You're out of uniform, soldier."

"No, it's just a different uniform these days, sir. I'm 12 years now with the NYPD, third in command of Operation Atlas. That's the anti-terrorism—"

"I know what Atlas is," Wilson interrupted. "I'm the one who requested your detail to secure BioWorld. That was 20 minutes ago. Nice of you to finally show up. Now, kindly get the hell out of my way—"

"Sorry, sir. No can do."

A blue armored personnel carrier with an image of a rearing cobra painted across its front rolled up to a stop at the top of the ramp.

"COBRA?" asked Wilson.

"Yessir: Chemical, Biological or Radiological Actions unit."

"I know what it stands for!" Wilson yelled from the car. "I invented the goddamn unit! What I want to know is why it's *here*."

"Because of the radiation traces, sir. Lots of 'em all over the street, the ramp, and especially the garage door you just drove out of—the entire place is a freakin' hot zone. We have to search the building for dirty bombs . . . and sorry to report, sir, we have to search your vehicle and everything inside."

At the top of the ramp, the door of the COBRA carrier flew upward, as if the jaws of the painted snake had snapped open.

A team dressed in yellow radiation suits moved quickly down the ramp, each carrying a halogen Geiger counter that emitted high-pitched warning beeps, like a truck backing up.

"Listen to that, sir. It's contaminated here, and I have to order—"

"Listen to *me,* Captain. See that smoking bridge across the river? It could have been taken out by a dirty bomb. That means fallout everywhere around here. On top of that, we're being bombarded by the biggest solar storm in 150 years. There's no way you'll get anything close to an accurate radiation reading today—especially not in this neighborhood. Now kindly get out of my way."

"I've considered all that, but with respect, General, the garage door you came through seems particularly hot, and I have to insist—"

"That *door* can only be opened by a control panel in Conrad Dinnick's private penthouse suite. Now, his close friends— the mayor, the governor, and the *President of the United States—* don't think he's hiding nukes in here, and neither do I. Do *you?"*

"Again, with all respect, sir, none of that matters. The city's Office of Emergency Management is in that building. If there's a radiation trail leading to it, I have to—"

"Listen, Crighton, I showed you my Homeland Security ID, I have security clearance higher than you can imagine, *and* I'm still a general in the U.S. Army. I'm issuing you a direct order to—"

A halogen Geiger counter by the garage door interrupted him with an ear-splitting shriek.

"Sir, that door is hotter than a thousand-dollar hooker," Crighton said. "There must be—"

Just then, the ground shook beneath a dozen fire engines as the trucks raced up York Avenue toward the Queensboro Bridge, distracting both Crighton and his men.

Wilson seized the moment to leap from the car. "I ordered you to stand down, Crighton," he hissed, pressing the long barrel of a silver-plated pistol against the sergeant's temple. "Now before we have a bloodbath, tell your men to lower their weapons while we talk."

The noise of the fire engines faded. Wilson cocked the hammer of his pistol. The officers surrounding the limo raised their weapons, and the ramp echoed with the clicking of the pump-action shotguns.

"Hold your fire, but maintain your positions!" Crighton ordered his men. "If he fires his weapon . . . kill him."

"The solar storm has knocked out communications, and without electronic communications, there's no way to know what's happening. We could be at war, Crighton," Wilson barked at him.

"Yes, sir, but it's still my duty to trace all radiation trails."

"You have no idea what's going on here, son."

"Sir, as an NYPD sergeant and unit leader—"

"You're a West Point grad, Crighton. You know the reasons we fought in Iraq—to protect our constitutional rights—the freedoms we all have under the writ of habeas corpus?"

"Of course I do . . . why are you giving me a history quiz with a gun to my head?" Crighton said through gritted teeth.

"No, Crighton, a *current-events* quiz. Tell your men about the only time habeas corpus can legally be suspended."

"Sir, I don't understand what you want me to—"

"The U.S. Constitution, Crighton! Article 1, Section 9. When does military authority supersede civilian authority?"

"Sir?"

"Answer me. Say the goddamned words."

"In cases of rebellion or invasion."

"*In cases of rebellion or invasion.* In case you haven't noticed, Crighton, we're at war. The infidels are at our gates—"

"Infidels?"

"The godless, suicide-bombing terrorists, Crighton. You're as blind and stupid as everyone at the Pentagon. For the last time, I am on a Code Red mission. Millions of lives are at stake, and you're in my way."

"I have my orders, sir."

"I'm giving you *new* orders. For all we know, this city could be under martial law. Under Article 1, Section 9, and the provisions of the Terrorism Prevention Act, I'm taking command of your unit. Now, order your men to fall back and clear this ramp, or so help me God, I'll put a bullet in your brain in three seconds. One, two . . ."

"Lower your weapons. Stand down. Do it!" Crighton shouted to his men. "I'm relinquishing command to General Wilson."

The officers lowered their guns and stepped aside as the COBRA vehicle backed off the ramp.

Wilson removed his pistol from Crighton's head.

"That's what it's all about, Crighton—the chain of command. Your orders are to secure the Tower's perimeter. All essential personnel have been escorted in; all non-essential personnel are gone. The building is in 24-hour lockdown until we ascertain the current threat level. No door or window can be opened—it's airtight and impenetrable. You'd need a goddamn nuke to get inside there now, son. Guard it with your life, and try to stay alive." Wilson clapped the soldier on the back, said, "Nice seeing you again, Crighton," and hopped back in the limo.

The car was off the ramp and heading south on York Avenue before Wilson had tucked his gun into its holster.

"You play a lot of games with people," Daniel ventured, as the general settled back into his seat and pulled a briefcase onto his lap.

"I don't play games, son. I give orders, and soldiers—even ex-soldiers—obey. That's what we program them to do."

Daniel looked at Wilson doubtfully. "But the chopper?"

"It should have returned for us. Whatever happened to the chopper wasn't because my orders weren't followed."

"And the bridge. Why?"

"Necessary diversionary tactic."

"Those people were innocent . . ."

"Unavoidable. Collateral damage." Wilson was stoic.

"It . . . doesn't seem—"

"Seem what? Right? Fair? Remember, my boy, all is fair in war, and this is war," Wilson said.

"But, *Dad* . . . I mean . . . I'm sorry . . ."

"It's all right, I understand that you're a little confused. It's okay to call me Dad if you want. You know you're like a son to me."

Daniel sighed heavily, then looked at his watch. "We'll never make it."

"We'll make it if there aren't any more goddamned delays. Traveling over ground makes the timing very tight, but we'll make it."

Wilson leaned toward the driver. "Slap that flashing light on the roof, and take 42nd Street across town. The police will have shut it down for emergency vehicles only. When we get to the Lincoln Tunnel, take the north tube—it's the shortest route across the river."

Turning back to Daniel, he opened the briefcase.

"Look at it. It's a beauty. I made it myself—C4 packing, random alpha-cryptic trip-wire protection and satellite phone detonator. It's guaranteed to satisfy. The only thing I didn't bank on is a solar storm messing up our satellite system. What are the chances of being hit by one of those today of all days?"

"Astronomical," Daniel said sardonically.

"But it won't be a problem; the phone has a roving trigger that's programmed to continually attempt an uplink—as soon as the first functional satellite comes online, it'll bounce the signal back here, and we'll have a connection. Then all we do is flip this," Wilson explained, pointing to a gold switch attached to the phone.

"Once that's done, the clock starts ticking down. Thirty minutes later, it will take out the primary target, and then the briefcase will self-destruct. I've put enough plastic explosives in this case to take out a city block, so we have to make sure we're in the air and on our way to South America when the timer reaches T-minus zero. Once the switch is flipped, nothing can stop it except for a disconnection code that only I know."

"But maybe . . . it won't work. Because of the storm. Maybe it's not supposed to work."

"Not *supposed* to work?!" Wilson shouted incredulously. "Supposing has nothing to do with it. This is a military operation, and I'm a military expert, son. Just sit back, enjoy the ride, and have a little faith."

CHAPTER 19

THE PICKUP SKIDDED ACROSS THE GREAT LAWN, its rear tires spitting chunks of turf through the air.

Frank crossed the quarter-mile-long field in less than a minute—more than enough time to see that the city had changed. Manhattan was suddenly defined by the black cloud drifting westward across its skyline, and by the police helicopters buzzing over the island. The scene reminded Frank of his last tour in Iraq when he'd been clearing cluster bombs from a playground and his squad leader had stepped on a land mine. There was a look on his face during the split second between the clicking of the mine's trigger and the man's realization that he was going to be blown to bits that haunted Frank to this day. It was the same look he saw now, etched on the faces of everyone he passed in the park: the hot dog vendor, the nanny pushing the stroller, the dad piggybacking his son, the old lady feeding pigeons.

It was the look of terror.

The memories of September 11, 2001, locked tight in the minds of so many New Yorkers, burst open and flooded the city with the horror of history repeating itself almost six years later.

From the corner of his eye, Frank could see Samantha signaling to him. Her eyelids were barely open, but she was holding her left arm in front of her, insistently pointing at something through the windshield.

"The castle in the sky, Daddy," she said weakly.

Frank was focused on navigating through the human stampede sweeping across the park. There were now hundreds of people running over the lawn, desperate to reach shelter, get to their homes, and find their families. He was certain that his daughter was hallucinating.

"Sure, Sammy, I see it, floating way up there. Now close your eyes and get some rest. We'll be home soon."

"No, Franklin . . . look up at the castle in the sky! We used to come here all the time with Mommy."

She was right. There it was, towering before them: Belvedere Castle. A medieval fortress in the heart of Manhattan, perched on top of a granite cliff—the highest point in Central Park. He'd taken Sarah and Samantha there for Sunday-afternoon picnics to, as Sarah loved to say, "dine like royalty with the richest but least expensive view in the city."

Perfect spot for a sniper nest, Frank thought, surveying the walkway on top of the castle wall. He spotted them instantly: at least six camouflaged soldiers with high-powered rifles taking position in the castle's battlements.

Great! A pickup truck driven by a wanted man, fleeing a chopper crash at high speed across a crowded public park. I might as well draw a bull's-eye on the roof. Not only am I a dead-easy target, I'm a justifiable kill. And at this distance, even these weekend warriors couldn't miss.

"Daddy?"

"Sammy, *not now.*"

"But I need to tell you something."

"*What?* I'm trying to drive."

"I decided I want you to sprinkle my ashes from the top of the castle—"

"*Samantha!* If you mention dying one more time, I swear to God I'll—"

"Thought you didn't believe in God, Frank," Samantha said sarcastically.

"Mock me later," Frank told her, flooring the gas pedal and sending the truck hurtling straight toward the pond beneath the castle.

He swerved to the right at the last minute onto a pedestrian walkway leading out of the park, laying on his horn, which screamed as he sped down the crowded path. Frank glanced at his daughter and said, "If you feel like praying again, Sammy, this would be a good time. Pray I don't hit anyone, because I'm sure as hell not slowing down."

The Dodge shot on to Central Park West, which was hopelessly jammed with cars and pedestrians fighting to get home, unable to move in any direction. A female traffic cop, who'd cleared a narrow path in the gridlock for an approaching ambulance, motioned for Frank to stop. He ignored her, plowing across the busy intersection to West 81st Street, forcing the cop to dive out of the way to avoid being mowed down. Even so, she knocked against the side of the truck as she jumped, cursing at Frank as she hit the ground.

"Oops," Frank said, seeing the cop in his sideview mirror stand up, brush herself off, and flip him the finger. Then he spotted the banners hanging over 81st Street.

Finally, a stroke of luck! The entire street had been closed off in preparation for a sidewalk festival. Frank cut through a line of pedestrians and smashed through a thicket of metal police barricades.

"We've done it, sweetie! We've got an open route west clear across town. If 11th Avenue isn't blocked, we'll be in the tunnel in 12, maybe 15 minutes, tops. That was some good praying, Sammy. Way to go, girl!"

"Not *that* good, Franklin. You nearly ran over a policewoman."

"I didn't run over anyone."

"Yes, you did."

"I did not."

"Did."

"Well . . . I didn't run her *over* . . . I just clipped her. If the city doesn't get blown to hell today, she can claim whiplash and take a six-month disability vacation in Florida. See? I did her a favor."

"*Dad!*"

"Sorry, Sammy. I could have hurt her; it's nothing to joke about. I'm just nervous. But I can't believe you're busting my chops. One second you're quiet, the next you're citing me for traffic violations."

"I feel a bit better . . . but I don't know about them."

"Them who?"

"Back there," Samantha said, jerking her thumb over her left shoulder like a hitchhiker, toward the bed of the truck.

"Oh shit, shit, shit!" Frank cried, remembering his unwanted cargo.

Then he spotted the police roadblock two blocks ahead.

Damn it, he realized, *I'll never get past them with two blood-covered crash victims in the back.*

He slammed on the brakes, reached under the seat for one of the detective's guns he'd stashed, and jumped out of the truck.

Then man he'd rescued had made a mattress for his female companion using fertilizer bags, tucking a small roll of sod under her head for a pillow.

She was unconscious, but Frank saw that her breathing was regular and deep.

"Thanks for picking us up," the man said.

Frank pointed the gun at him. "Two questions, and don't even think about lying to me," he barked. "Who the hell are you, and why was the military chasing down your chopper?"

"My name is Dinnick, I'm the—"

"*Dinnick?*" Despite the mask of dried blood plastering the man's face, Frank now recognized his wealthy employer. "I know who you are, Mr. Dinnick. Why were they after you?"

"I honestly don't know *who's* after me anymore."

"Well, you better come up with something fast."

"Maybe you don't know about the attack," Conrad said, emphatically, "or at least, about the explosion at the Queensboro Bridge. Half the bridge is in the water, and the Re-Creation Center I built on Roosevelt Island is completely destroyed. So I think—"

"That was the explosion I heard? The bridge . . . the Re-Creation Center, destroyed?"

"That's right. They must be shutting down airspace over Manhattan like after 9/11, and . . . look, it's too complicated. I work with the Army, with the government. Someone in my company, or terrorists or a foreign government . . . *someone's* trying to kill me because of something I know. I don't have time to explain it all to you. I said I'd give you $100,000 to take me to Hoboken. Put the gun away, and I'll make it $200,000. You have no idea how high the stakes are—"

"Well, aren't you generous, Mr. Dinnick. You already *owe* me $200,000 for landscaping your island, and I'm still waiting for the check, pal."

"I had no idea who you—"

"Never mind," Frank said, waving the gun toward Katherine. "Who's she?"

"A psychic."

"Oh, of course, a *psychic*. Who else would you drop out of the sky with? Wait—she's that TV psychic . . . Katherine what's-her-name, the one freaking everyone out on the radio with bomb threats . . . on *your* radio station, right?"

Frank pressed the gun against Conrad's ribs. "I don't know what kind of sick game you're playing here, but pick up your girlfriend right now and haul your trillionaire ass out of my truck before I blow a hole in—"

"Daddy!"

Samantha had slid open the small rear window and was staring at them. The dirty frame accented the dark circles under her eyes and the paleness of her face.

Frank immediately hid the gun behind his back.

"Sammy, I swear I'm not going to hurt anyone else, but we've got to get to your aunt's right away. We can't take these people—"

"Mommy says to take them with us."

"*What?*"

"Mommy just talked to me. Stop looking at me like that—she did, really. She said we all have to go together."

"Okay, honey, that's good. Now shut the window and fasten your seat belt. We're leaving in a hurry."

Samantha closed the window and dropped out of sight, and Frank turned back to Conrad.

"I don't want to hurt you, but I will. It looks like the Army's after you, and I *know* the police are after me, so we don't make a good team. Now get out. You see how sick my little girl looks, she's delirious—"

"She's dying."

"What did you just say?"

"Chronic genocalimic leukemia, right?"

"How the hell did you know that?"

"Because I went to med school, and I'm a geneticist. I can't promise you, but I think I could help her—"

"You could what? You lying bastard."

"If you know who I am, then you must know what I do. There's a new gene therapy I'm developing. It's still in trials, but I think it could reverse the disease."

"I don't believe you."

"Your oncologist must have told you what I can see just by looking at her face: She's got weeks, maybe only days. Get me to Hoboken, and I'll do what I can for her, I swear. I've developed a new treatment. I'll have a team of doctors working with her day and night."

"What the hell is in Hoboken?"

"In the right hands, global protection. In the wrong hands . . . a new virus that could kill a million New Yorkers in a month. I told you, I do work for the government—I develop vaccines to protect us against biological attacks. Get me to my lab, and I'll help your daughter."

"If you're lying to me, I'll kill you."

"If that bug gets loose, I'll be *begging* you to kill me."

The two men stared at each other for a second.

"It's a deal. I don't know if they'll let us past the roadblock up ahead, but I'm going through one way or the other," Frank said, tucking the gun into the waistband of his jeans.

He stuck out his hand and shook Conrad's hand. "Frank Dell," he offered cautiously.

"Conrad Dinnick," Conrad replied.

"Looks like we're both trying to do the same thing—save lives," Frank said, pulling one of the detective's badges from his back pocket and handing it to Conrad. "Take this. When they stop us at the roadblock, show it to them and say your name is Big Davie."

"I don't need a badge," Conrad said, pulling a wallet from his pants pocket. "I have top Pentagon clearance and a Class-10 Homeland Security pass. If we needed to, we could walk into the Oval Office for tea."

"Let's just hope we can get into the Lincoln Tunnel."

Upon hearing the word *tunnel,* Katherine stirred in the back of the truck. Now semiconscious, she began softly mumbling. Neither of the men could hear her, and even if they had, they wouldn't have been unable to understand what she was saying: *Tunnel . . . limo . . . virus . . . Sarah . . . twins.*

Samantha was asleep when Frank climbed back behind the wheel. Conrad's pass got them through the police on West 81st Street with no problem. They headed south down 11th Avenue, the Hudson River on their right. Frank looked across the river at the condos going up along Hoboken's abandoned piers, and farther south toward the little patch of green he seeded once a year called Frank Sinatra Park.

Conrad's pass got them through six more police checkpoints. They made it all the way to the Lincoln Tunnel's north tube entrance in less than 15 minutes.

A National Guardsman shook his head while inspecting the truck and its disheveled occupants, but waved them past after checking out Conrad's credentials.

The white tiles on the tunnel wall had yellowed, like the

teeth of a lifelong smoker. They reminded Frank of the YMCA swimming pool he'd gone to when he was Samantha's age. Swimming made him feel like he was weightless, practically flying—the way he felt now looking at his daughter and wondering if Conrad really could heal her.

Samantha met his gaze, flashing him a dimmer version of her thousand-watt smile. She saw her mother again, standing at the entrance of the tunnel as they moved underground and beneath the river. Sarah was smiling as always, and the weary girl heard her say, *Soon, Sammy, very soon.*

"I'm going home, Daddy."

"I think so, baby. I think maybe you're right. There *is* a God, and She just answered our prayers."

CHAPTER 20

"I NEED TO KNOW . . . IS HE . . . IS MY FATHER DEAD?" Daniel asked haltingly.

"Turn on the all-news station," Wilson commanded the driver.

A male voice vibrated through the limo's speakers. The announcer grew increasingly emotional and incoherent as he described the events unfolding around him.

" . . . we just don't know how many people have been hurt or killed, but the bridge has collapsed, it's collapsed! Rescue workers are trying to reach the island, but the fire . . . the fire is so big . . . oh God! . . . it's 9/11 all over again . . . it must be another terrorist attack . . . there's no other—"

There was a sudden thud, as though the microphone had been knocked over, and then a calm female voice began reporting.

"You're listening to Action News Radio. There have been erroneous reports of a terrorist attack in the city, but this has not, I repeat, not been confirmed. The facts we know so far are as follows: Approximately half an hour ago a massive explosion on Roosevelt Island damaged or destroyed much of the Queensboro Bridge. As of yet, there has been no public statement from the mayor, governor, or police commissioner.

"Fire Commissioner Erwin Douglas says that so far the explosions seem to be related to a rupture in a large natural gas line on the island.

No group or individual has claimed responsibility for the explosions.

"Police anti-terrorism units and the New York National Guard are patrolling the city, but they say that there's no sign of any type of ongoing terrorist attack.

"So, although the situation may look chaotic in the streets right now, the most important thing is not to panic, folks. This appears to be an accident—not an attack. Stay tuned to Action News Radio for up-to-the-minute coverage of this breaking news story."

A sudden burst of static shot through the limo, and the driver moved to turn the volume down.

"Leave it on," Wilson ordered. He opened his briefcase and checked the satellite phone. "No connection yet."

The newscaster continued. *"What's even more frightening is the ongoing solar storm, which is making it difficult for New Yorkers to use their phones or the Internet to communicate. Again, this is not due to terrorism. It is, believe it or not, a weather-related problem, although it's quite a serious one. People are advised not to look at the sun, as sudden bursts of light during severe solar storms have been known to cause blindness, burn skin, and even start forest fires. The storm has already damaged scores of communication satellites. More than 300 of our sister radio and television stations across the country have been knocked off the air. If the same thing happens to us, do not adjust your dial. We're told that the disruptions will be intermittent, and likely temporary. Again, we urge you: Stay tuned to Action News Radio for up-to-the-minute coverage.*

"Now, recapping the facts. What we know so far is that approximately 35 minutes ago, a large explosion on Roosevelt Island destroyed much of the Queensboro Bridge. The new BioWorld Supercomputer Re-Creation Center under the bridge, which was scheduled to open today, has been completely destroyed. A fire at the site, at the moment believed to be from a ruptured gas main, is burning out of control. Several hundred people had assembled for the center's opening ceremony, but remarkably, we've received no reports of casualties so far, although that could change. . . . We just don't know at the moment."

The limo was moving west across 42nd Street when hundreds of anxious-looking people began to pour into the street from Grand Central Station. Police pushed the crowds back onto the sidewalk as emergency vehicles flew down the road toward the East Side.

"The subways are emptying—" Wilson remarked to Daniel.

"Sir," the driver interrupted Wilson nervously, "the road's getting so crowded that I'm having a hard time getting around these people."

"I don't care if you drive *over* them. You've got 20 minutes to get to the Jersey side of the Lincoln tunnel. Turn on the siren and flasher, and *move!*"

When the limo's siren began wailing, several police officers stepped out on the road and opened a clear path. The car began speeding through Midtown toward the Hudson River.

And on the radio: *"We have another breaking development: Subways in all five New York boroughs are being evacuated as a precautionary measure. Once again, there's no, I repeat, no confirmation of a terrorist attack—just a lot of confusion and, naturally, anxiety.*

"We're still waiting for a news conference with the mayor, governor, and police commissioner . . . but . . . what? We've just received a report that the mayor and governor may have been on the Roosevelt Island Tram when the bridge collapsed, but there's no word on their whereabouts or condition, although some fear that they must be seriously, or fatally, injured. I apologize for the vagueness of the report . . . the solar storm is making any form of communication with officials or our reporters in the field virtually impossible. . . . It's like we're being thrown back in time."

"It sounds like the beginning of the end," Wilson said wryly, as the limo crossed 8th Avenue.

Daniel looked up and saw the giant neon signs of Times Square that were filled with images of the day's news. First there were the pictures of the burning Queensboro Bridge, then some of the mayor and governor, followed by an image of his father. Then there they were—he and Michael, a 40-foot high photograph of the Dinnick brothers—being broadcast above the world's busiest intersection.

Daniel was startled by seeing his brother's face in front of him so suddenly, staring at him like a ghost from above. *What is that expression on his face?* Daniel wondered in disbelief, his heart beginning to race. *It's accusation . . . he's accusing me . . . he's blaming me!*

His mind drifted back to the day in BioWorld's Hoboken lab, when everything between the two brothers changed. He felt like he was watching a movie of a moment in his life being played back for him: Daniel walking in on Michael . . . catching him conducting experiments on himself, using a hypodermic air gun to inject cloned human embryo cells into his brain stem.

"What you're doing is wrong. Not only could it kill you . . . it's a crime against God," Daniel had said, threatening to go to their father to report his brother. Michael had been laughing and laughing—so smug—mocking Daniel.

"Go ahead, go to Dad and report me. But while you're at it, tell him about all the BioWorld money, the hundreds of millions of dollars that *someone* has been diverting to supply developing countries with free antiviral drugs—drugs that BioWorld should be *selling* on the open market for profit. They call that theft, embezzlement, larceny—take your pick. It's just the kind of thing Dad would love to hear about."

"I don't know how you know about that, but it's different. I'm trying to help millions of people. I'm doing God's work," Daniel had explained.

"So am I, Danny, just in a very different way. Now if you want to keep doing what you're doing, you'll let me do what *I'm* doing. So it's our little secret, agreed?"

"All right . . . for the common good."

"For the common good," Michael had repeated. Then he held up the hypodermic gun and walked toward Daniel, saying, "There's just one other condition I have. . . ."

Everything was fuzzy after that—sickness . . . a tumor . . . and Wilson, helping out, covering something up . . . what was it? *What had happened?*

He pulled back from his daydream as the image of his

father's face flashed back on the screen.

"Dad?" Daniel asked, staring through the window then turning to Wilson.

"With the phones out and satellites down, there's no way to be sure *exactly* what happened to him, but I think we both know," Wilson told Daniel. "But remember that whatever happened, we agreed it was for the best," Wilson said, closing the briefcase.

"Right . . . for the best . . . but the vaccine—there isn't enough . . . not yet . . . not for everyone."

"We don't need it for everyone, and as long as we can re-create it, there's not a problem," Wilson reassured him.

As the car pulled onto the ramp for the tunnel, the female newscaster's professional delivery evaporated, developing a hysterical edge.

"Oh my God . . . we've just received a confirmed report that . . ."

The radio fizzled out completely.

A group of National Guard soldiers were lined up along the entrance of the Lincoln Tunnel as the limo descended the ramp to the north tube. A group of soldiers approached the limo, brandishing M16 machine guns.

"Authorized personnel only," said one of the soldiers as others inspected the underside of the limo with long-handled mirrors.

Wilson produced his identification. "Here's my authorization."

The soldier saluted, saying, "Go ahead, General, sir."

As they passed into the tunnel, the speakers began crackling again.

"We're losing radio transmission. The storm's knocking everything out," Wilson said.

The reporter's voice began cutting in and out. *". . . all tunnels and bridges leading in and out of the city are being closed until—"*

The radio died completely.

Wilson leaned forward and put his mouth next to the driver's ear.

"This tunnel is just under a mile-and-a-half long, then it's a three-mile drive to Hoboken. There's a group of people waiting for us there, the kind of people you don't keep waiting. If we don't meet them in exactly 15 minutes, it's likely we'll all be dead . . . and I'll make sure you're the first to go."

CHAPTER 21

JACK TWISTED THE HARLEY'S THROTTLE BACK until the roar of the engine almost deafened them, and then popped the clutch. The chopper's front wheel jumped off the ground, the rear tire screeched against the pavement, and the bike shot forward at a gut-wrenching speed.

"Whoa!" Zoe yelled, the acceleration whipping her against the backrest, nearly spilling her onto the street.

She grabbed Jack's leather jacket, then slid her arms around his waist.

"Never been on a Harley before?" Jack yelled to her.

"Believe it or not it's—"

"What? Can't hear you."

Zoe put her lips against Jack's right ear. "I said, believe it or not, it's my first time on a motorbike."

"*A motorbike?* What are ya, British?" Jack asked in his thickest Brooklyn accent.

"*Excuse me*—I've never been on a motor*cycle* before, and for the record, I'm a Joisey girl."

"From New Jersey *and* a reporter?"

"Yeah, well, nobody's perfect."

Jack swerved to miss a pothole, and Zoe shrieked.

"Listen—don't be scared," he assured her. "We'll only get into trouble if you tense up. Try to relax, don't fight the motion, and just follow the movement of my body. When I turn right, you lean right. If I turn left, you lean left. Don't worry, you won't fall off . . . and always keep your feet on the foot pegs. I'll be moving fast, cutting through heavy traffic and taking a few shortcuts, so hang on tight. Get it?"

"Got it."

In spite of the heat, Zoe was trembling violently. She pressed herself against Jack's body and tightened her arms around his midsection. She could feel his solid stomach muscles through the thick leather and began calculating his age.

What am I doing? she wondered. It dawned on her that she hadn't been this physically close to a man since the day she quit the beauty-pageant circuit.

"Hey, you're really squeezing the breath out of me!" Jack yelled over his shoulder.

"Oh, sorry," Zoe said, embarrassed. She tried to release her grip but couldn't. Jack's left hand had wrapped around her interlaced fingers and held them in place for a second.

Jack laughed, "No, you gotta hold on tight. I just meant, you're really strong, that's all. I don't mind, I'm just surprised, 'cause, you know, you're kind of petite . . . I mean . . . you must, you know, work out a lot or something."

"Boxing."

"Say what?" Jack shouted.

Zoe put her mouth against his ear again. "I said, I box for exercise. I'm a boxer."

"A boxer? What? Like Rocky Balboa?" Jack laughed.

"Yeah, just like Rocky," Zoe replied, surprised to find herself laughing as well.

"So if you're a boxer, why'd you need a stun gun to take out a broken-down old man like me?"

"You had a gun! You were acting crazy—oh, sorry . . . but you were—"

"Fuhgettaboutit, I deserved it. I guess I am a little crazy. Besides, I haven't felt anything that intense since . . . well, in a long, long time."

Zoe paused, squeezing her arms around him a little tighter. "You're not an old man."

"Say what?"

"I said, I'm cold, really cold . . . man," Zoe answered, realizing she couldn't stop shivering.

"CIS."

"What?"

"Critical Incident Stress. Your body's trying to protect itself. Your blood pressure's dropped, so you feel cold. Basically, you're in shock. You just saw some horrible shit back there, but I can't do anything for you right now. Just hold on tight, kid, and try to keep warm against me. If you get dizzy, tell me right away."

"What? You go to medical school before becoming a cop?"

"Nah . . . my son's a . . . my son was a paramedic."

"Yeah? What's he doing now?"

"I can't talk about it. Gotta focus on the road."

Zoe sensed she'd opened a deep wound.

"I'm sorry," Zoe said, and was silent for a moment. Then, in a soft voice: "I know what it's like to lose a child."

It was the first time she'd ever said that out loud; she wasn't sure why she'd said it or even if Jack had heard her. She began shivering more violently and held Jack tighter, pressing her face against his back. Until she realized his leather jacket was wet, she hadn't even known she'd been crying.

As they began turning west, away from the East River and toward the tunnel, Zoe took a last look over her shoulder at the broken, smoldering bridge. Then she closed her eyes and kept them shut until she stopped crying.

Jack was true to his word: His riding was fast, furious, and dangerous—mounting sidewalks and terrorizing pedestrians one minute, and suddenly cutting in front of a bus the next. He headed the wrong way down one-way streets, played chicken with oncoming traffic, and ignored stop signs and traffic lights.

Within five minutes, they were in the heart of Midtown.

Zoe opened her eyes and was amazed at what she saw. They were less than a dozen blocks from the burning bridge, yet no one seemed to know what had happened to their city. As always, the streets were filled with people, some had even stopped walking and were looking up at the smoke in the eastern sky. But there was no panic, no screaming, no run-for-your-life hysteria.

Just like September 11th, she thought. *They don't know, just like I didn't know.*

Even a hardcore news junkie like Zoe had been late to catch on about the significance of 9/11. She'd been scheduled to fly to Albany to report on a mob-related Supreme Court hearing and was sitting on the stoop of her uptown apartment waiting for an airport limo, sipping coffee and reading *The Trumpet,* when the first plane hit. When the second one hit, she was still reading the paper, wondering why her car was so late.

She found out that the city was under attack when the limo dispatcher called on her cell phone explaining that her car would be delayed due to bad traffic downtown.

That had always stuck in her mind: *Delay due to bad traffic downtown.*

"Yeah, so, this is New York. Traffic's always bad," Zoe had answered.

"Yes, Miss, that's true . . . but the planes crashing into the World Trade Center have really fouled things up—"

"What?!" Zoe had yelled, only then noticing the smoke rising over Lower Manhattan.

She got on her bicycle and pedaled like crazy. She was only blocks from the World Trade Center when the South Tower came down, the dust storm blowing her off the bike and into a story she would cover for the next year. Despite the pain and loss she'd reported on, she tried to never let it get to her. She threw herself into her work, determined to beat the competition and get the most heartrending stories possible.

The Trumpet offered free trauma-therapy sessions for reporters who'd covered the events, but Zoe didn't attend any of them. She'd dealt with what she'd seen that day in the same way she'd dealt with her so-called mother: She turned her back and left it in the past, where it could never hurt her again.

But everything she'd walked away from was beginning to seep into her heart and mind now as she sped through the streets of Manhattan after another catastrophe, entrusting her life to a crazy man she'd just met during what amounted to a shoot-out.

She now remembered that it was after 9/11 when she first heard of Katherine Haywood. Someone in her office had a friend who'd seen the psychic pass out during a group reading three days before the attack, then wake up with a splitting headache—and a premonition of an airplane crash in lower Manhattan.

At the time, Zoe dismissed the rumor as the self-promotion of an opportunistic businesswoman trying to tap in to a market of bereaved New Yorkers. But years later, after she'd been assigned to the Your Lucky Stars column, Zoe had come across two others who'd been at that same reading. Both of them—one a doctor, the other a district attorney—swore that Katherine had predicted the terrorist attack.

Oh God, I've done everything I possibly could to screw this woman's reputation in my columns, and she might have been telling the truth all along? Zoe wondered.

"Jack," she suddenly yelled, "do you think maybe this psychic is for real?"

"What? Not a chance."

"But how could she have known about the explosion? And the things she said to Dinnick, things she just had no way of knowing . . . the tram, the explosions. How do explain that?"

"*I'm* supposed to be the crazy one, not you."

"No, but really, what if she's the real deal? What if it's possible that the people we love are really still around, and someone like Katherine can talk to them?"

"Listen, all I know is what I know: When you're dead, you're dead."

Zoe pressed close to Jack again, this time whispering urgently, "Hurry, Jack, please."

Jack revved the engine higher, weaving like a drunk through the busy streets.

They raced across Midtown in what had to be record time, even for a cop. But when they reached Times Square, they abruptly stopped.

News of the explosion had spread slowly at first, creeping beneath the radar, before exploding in a burst of panic that infected the center of the city with desperation. It was like New Year's Eve without the celebration.

Hundreds of people jammed the streets, trying to hail taxis that couldn't move, and flocking to subway entrances already packed with commuters evacuating the underground stations.

Police and military vehicles cordoned off the square as helicopters hovered overhead. Pictures of the burning bridge flashed everywhere—on massive digital billboards, on the television display screens of discount electronics stores, and embedded in the news crawlers snaking along the facades of building after building.

"We'll never get out of this mess," Zoe said.

"Oh, yes we will!" Jack shouted. "Don't you worry, I'm going to get you through this. I won't let anything happen to you, kid. The cops will have cleared out 42nd Street as an emergency route—that's just two blocks south of here. Hold on!"

Jack revved the bike, popped over the curb and through the gate of a construction site, crossed 43rd Street, and headed in to a parking lot that emptied out onto West 42nd.

He tore down the street, just ahead of the roadblocks that were being set up. Jack knew that the Lincoln Tunnel would likely be shut down, but that the north tube would be reserved for police and fire department use, so that's where he headed.

He rode down the ramp and stopped behind a black limo being checked out by a squad of National Guard soldiers.

Two NYPD officers carrying 9mm Glocks approached the motorcycle, and a pair of National Guardsmen aimed machine guns at Jack and Zoe from the tunnel entrance.

"Back off, back off now!" one of the officers shouted at

Jack, his pistol pointed at Jack's chest.

"Don't move, don't even twitch," Jack muttered to Zoe, and then yelled out, "I'm a cop . . . can I open my jacket to show you my shield?"

"Move slow, real slow," the officer cautioned. His partner stood back, keeping his gun aimed at Zoe.

Jack opened his jacket just enough to display the badge attached to his belt. The lead cop approached him hesitantly, and then said, "Jack? Is that really you?"

"Yeah . . . hey, Bobby, how ya doing, man?"

"Not so good today," said the cop, lowering his gun. "Can't believe we're going through this hell again. Hey, I thought they bounced you for messing up that priest's face."

"Nah, just stuck me under a mountain of paper. I been working cold cases for the last 100 years."

"Well, better than still pounding a beat at 50."

"So can we go through? I've got a suspect I really need to question in Hoboken."

"Sorry, Jack, nobody's allowed through the tunnel unless they have a military pass."

"Come on, Bobby, cut me some slack. I'm following up on a lead in Jersey that could connect with this mess. I gotta follow up. I'd call the feds in, but none of the damn phones are working."

"Sorry, man, they're making no exceptions. The National Guard's calling the shots on this one. You believe this? Nearly 30 years on the force, and I'm taking orders from some Army brat with zits on his face."

"I hear ya, pal. Hey, how's your boy doing? Still with the hook and ladder?"

"Yeah, yeah. Get this: The kid's a captain now, running his own firehouse. Remember when he and Liam used to play in your backyard and . . . uh, Jack, I'm real sorry. It's been so long since I've seen you. We were all torn up about Liam—"

"Thank you," Jack answered abruptly, looking down. "This mess kind of brings it all right back."

"Don't you know it. My stomach flipped when I heard the

blast." Bobby looked Jack and Zoe over carefully, and then said, "You really got a lead on this—someone connected to this bridge thing?"

"Swear to Christ, Bobby. It's from a cold case I been working on, a bomb maker in Hoboken. I don't know if it'll pan out, but if it does, maybe it could save a couple of our boys from getting blown to hell."

"Yeah, I hear ya. But I like I said, the Guard's in charge now. I tell ya what . . . for old time's sake, I'll make it right with them. But before I stick my neck out, tell me something straight. Are you still crazy, Jack? I mean, riding around on that chopper like Peter freakin' Fonda?"

"No, man. I saw a shrink for years. I'm good. I swear to Christ, I'm on the job. The Harley's the best thing to get through traffic, that's all."

"Who's she?"

"Her? This is my girlfriend. Now, ask yourself: Could an old slob like me land a babe like her if I was crazy?"

"Good point."

"I just didn't want to leave her in the city with all that's happening."

Zoe leaned forward and kissed Jack on the cheek. "He *is* crazy—crazy in love," she said.

"Uh-huh. I think you're a little young for him, sweetheart, but what the hell, we could all be dead tomorrow, right? Wait here. And, Jack, take my advice, don't move till I come back."

Jack looked at the young soldiers nervously fingering their machine guns, and nodded his head. "You got it, Bobby."

"So, introducing me as your girlfriend already?" Zoe asked sarcastically, as Bobby walked over to the soldiers.

"Maybe I should have introduced you as a cop-bashing, lie-spinning, sleazeball tabloid reporter?"

"Ah, no—girlfriend was a good idea."

Jack saw Bobby arguing with the soldiers. "This could take some time," he said.

"Jack, I think we're just about out of time."

CHAPTER 22

FRANK SQUINTED THROUGH THE PICKUP'S CRACKED WINDSHIELD, trying to see beyond the mist rising up in front of him after he'd entered the tunnel.

It was the strangest thing he'd ever seen—as though they'd driven into a dense white cloud, visibility went from 100 percent to practically zero in seconds.

This is too weird . . . I can't see anything, Frank thought. *Nothing at all. Where in the hell are we?*

. . . there is no hell. Franklin, I love you . . .

I love you, too, Sarah, Frank thought, and then shook his head to clear the cobwebs.

What, am I hearing things now? he wondered, then looked at his daughter.

"Did you just say something to me, Sammy?"

"No, I didn't, but this fog is really cool, isn't it?"

"I wouldn't call it 'cool.' Are you sure you just didn't say something like 'There is no hell' . . . and 'I love you'?"

"No . . . I mean, yeah, I know there's no hell, and *of course* I love you . . . but I didn't say anything." Then she gave him a sudden look of excitement.

"Oh, Daddy, are you starting to hear God language, too?"

"What? 'God language'? No, Sammy. It's been a long, long day and . . . where the hell is this fog coming from?!" Frank shouted, confused by the strange mist, and angry that he was moving so slowly. He turned on his headlights, but the beams just bounced back into his eyes.

He rolled down the window and stuck his head out. The mist felt warm and soft against his face, like a caress. And the smell was so . . . sweet, like the fragrant jasmine potpourri Sarah used to leave all over the house in her hand-painted ceramic bowls.

Frank pulled his head back inside, thinking, *What is* this *stuff?*

They'd passed the halfway point of the tunnel, crossing the New York-New Jersey border, and were moving beneath the Hudson River, nearly a hundred feet underwater.

But the cloud, or fog, or whatever it was, kept closing in on them, tighter and tighter, until Frank couldn't see at all.

Thank God they've closed the tunnel, or we'd have had a head-on collision by now.

He knew that they had to be close to the New Jersey exit, but he had to slow the truck to a crawl.

"Hurry up, Daddy. They're waiting for us," Samantha said impatiently.

"Who's waiting?"

"All of them. . . ."

"Well, whoever you're talking about, Sammy, is going have to wait a little longer. This fog . . . I've never seen anything like it. I have to stop for a few minutes until it clears or I'll hit something."

Frank put on his hazard lights, pulled over to what he guessed was the side of the road, shifted to neutral, and killed the engine. He turned on the radio to see if he could get a report on where the tunnel fog was coming from, but there was only static. Then the radio died and the headlights went out. He tried to start the engine, but nothing happened.

Now the battery's dead? Frank looked at his daughter in confusion, and said, "Listen, Sammy, if you've got nothing else to pray about right at this moment, you might consider praying that no cars come up behind us because—"

But before he'd finished his sentence, they were rear-ended hard enough to push the truck down the tunnel several yards.

Frank's chest bounced off the steering wheel.

"Son of a bitch!" Frank yelled into the rearview mirror at the limousine that had plowed into them. His anger was instantly usurped by panic when he saw that Samantha had undone her seat belt just after the impact, slid onto the floor, and was now curled up in the fetal position.

Frank reached down, lifted her into his arms, and shouted, "Sammy! Sammy! Wake up! Please talk to me. Please, honey!"

Samantha's eyes were shut tight. He couldn't understand why she'd be unconscious—the collision had been a relatively minor one, not too much worse than a bad fender bender.

Frank shook her gently, tears welling up in his eyes. "Come on, Sammy," he pleaded. "For Daddy, please. Just open your eyes."

Her eyes opened. She focused on her father's face and smiled. "I'm okay, Daddy. I just had a really, really bad feeling about what's behind us, and I guess I got scared for a second. I'm all right now."

Frank laughed in relief, and kissed her all over her face and forehead.

"When I saw you lying on the floor, I got a bad feeling too," he said, instinctively checking her neck and collarbone for fractures. She seemed fine . . . more than fine. There was color in her face, and she was warmer than she'd been all day. He checked her pulse; it was strong and steady. In fact, she looked better and seemed livelier than she'd been in months.

"Do you hurt anywhere, honey? Your head? Your tummy? Your back?"

"No, Daddy. Like I said, I just got scared . . . and that scared me even more, because you know I'm almost never afraid."

"I know, Sammy. It's this fog we're stuck in. It feels so spooky."

"Oh, no, it wasn't the fog. The fog is friendly—it loves us. It's what hit us that's scary."

"The fog loves us? Whatever you say, kid. Can you sit tight for a minute? I have to check on our passengers in the back, and then I'll see who hit us to make sure they're not too evil, okay?"

"Okay, but please be careful."

As Frank stepped out of the truck, the lights running along the length of the tunnel's ceiling blinked out one at time, like a mile-and-a-half-long line of fluorescent dominoes disappearing into the distance. He should have been standing in complete darkness, but there was a pale glow emanating from the fog itself, as though the mist was charged with some kind of internal energy source.

This is absolutely freakin' weird, Frank thought, looking back at Samantha. Aloud, he told her, "Now I mean it, Sammy. You stay right there—don't move until I check things out."

"See ya later, alligator," Samantha laughed. "But everything is okay now. I just realized that we're safe. We're here . . . we're finally here."

We're stuck *here, that's for sure,* Frank realized, moving to the rear of the truck.

He looked into the back and saw Katherine and Conrad digging their way out from beneath a pile of turf.

"Everyone alive back here?" Frank asked, sticking his hands into a thick sod roll and shoving it aside.

"I think we're fine," Conrad said. "This grass really cushioned us. What did you hit?"

"I didn't hit anything; someone hit us," Frank said, already walking toward the limo that had stopped about 15 feet down the tunnel, and which was barely visible in the hazy light.

The hair on the back of his neck stood up, and his soldier's survival instincts went on high alert when he saw BIOWLD2 stamped on the license plate.

BioWorld? Why do these guys keep smashing into my life? Do I have the cops and *the BioWorld goons chasing me?*

When Frank got to the limo, he saw blood splattered on the inside of the windshield and the driver's body slumped over the wheel.

What the hell? Did he smash his head against the glass?

He tried the door, but it was locked. Then he began rapping on the window.

"Hey, buddy, you okay?" he asked.

The man didn't move. Frank leaned in closer and noticed a hole in the side of the driver's head, and a gun on the passenger seat.

Frank jumped back.

What's going on here? Why did this guy shoot himself? This is all too much. . . .

The rest of the limo's windows were darkly tinted, and all the doors were locked. Frank banged on the roof, but there was no reply.

He walked back to the pickup and found Conrad and Katherine kneeling on the truck bed, brushing dirt off each other.

"What happened?" Conrad asked Frank.

"You tell me. It was one of your damned security limos that smashed into us."

The truck's back window slid open, and Samantha's face appeared. She surveyed the back of the truck, then looked at Katherine and asked, "Are you Kathy?"

"Yes, I am," Katherine replied, crawling over to the window. She gently touched the little girl's face and asked, "Are you hurt, sweetheart?"

"Nope, just really, really sick."

"I know," Katherine said, grimacing for several seconds as a scorching pain passed through her body. "You've been hurting for a long time, haven't you?"

"Yeah, but my mom says it won't hurt much longer, and she said you'd help me."

"Your mom . . . Sarah, right?" As Katherine spoke the words, she remembered Italy and knew instantly that this little girl was the same one she'd seen in the vision that had pulled her back to New York.

"Yeah, Sarah's my mom," Samantha said.

"She's with us."

"She's been talking to me all day in God language."

"Well, now she's showing me a picnic basket. Do you know what that means?" Katherine asked.

Frank's hand landed heavily on Katherine's shoulder, and he pulled her away from the window.

"What are you talking to my daughter about?!" Frank shouted. He looked at Conrad angrily. "Who the hell does this woman think she is?"

"She's a psychic. She's . . . *odd*. Christ, I don't know anymore. I think she might even be on the level."

"Yeah, well, she should stay away from my daughter." Turning to Katherine, he fumed, "What do *you* know about Sarah?"

"Not much. I'm just feeling her energy now. She was funny and very kind, she gave herself to others, and she loved you— both of you—very deeply. I know that much. She's showing me an old potbelly stove . . . a Franklin stove . . . is that your name?" Katherine paused and looked Frank in the eye. "Do you have any idea how open your daughter's faith has made her to the spirit world?"

Frank stared in disbelief.

"I know how you feel, Frank," Conrad sympathized. "But she kind of grows on you after a while."

"Thanks a lot," Katherine said wryly. "But that's a pretty cheap compliment coming from a trillionaire."

"You're right, you deserve better," Conrad said, reaching over and pulling a clump of sod from her long red hair. Then he turned and looked out at the glowing ring of white mist surrounding them. "Where are we? What is all this fog?"

Katherine wasn't sure what it was, but she felt its energy penetrating her very being. It was the same feeling she'd get when she conducted a highly charged group reading.

"We're nearly through the tunnel, but the truck's battery is dead. We're going to have to walk out of here and hitch a ride to Hoboken," Frank told the others.

Then they heard a car door open, and General Wilson stepped out of the back of the limo, saying, "We're the only ones going to Hoboken. None of you are going anywhere—*ever!*" He had a briefcase in one hand and his silver pistol in the other.

"Wilson? What are you—I told you to stay in the BioWorld Tower, to stay with Daniel."

"I'm afraid the Tower will be closed for a century or so, Mr. Dinnick, and I *am* with Daniel . . . *sir.*"

The young man got out of the limo behind Wilson.

"Danny, why are you here? What's going on?" Conrad asked, completely perplexed.

"I've g-got . . . bad news . . . D-Dad."

Katherine climbed down from the truck, rubbing her eyes as she stared at Daniel—but the vision was still there. Superimposed just above his head was an image of the Archangel Michael.

"*Michael,*" she whispered.

CHAPTER 23

"YOU'RE A DIFFICULT MAN TO KILL, MR. DINNICK," Wilson said, pointing his gun at Conrad through the mist. "I should have taken care of you myself. I don't know how you survived the helicopter 'accident' I had planned for you, but I assure you, you won't escape this tunnel."

Frank moved forward, quickly placing himself between Wilson and Samantha.

"Nobody moves—including you, gardener, unless you want me to put your daughter out of her misery right now."

"Stay in the truck, sweetie," Frank ordered Samantha over his shoulder, never taking his eyes off the man with the gun. To him, Frank said, "I know you. You're General John Wilson . . . you got me hired to landscape the island."

"Affirmative, Sergeant Dell. Amazing how much the Army's simple psychological profile reveals about a person, isn't it? Yours just screamed *fall guy*. If our plans fouled up at any point, all we had to do was hang everything on you—the embittered explosives expert; an Islamic sympathizer, flat broke, with a dying daughter and extreme animosity toward the U.S. government for killing his wife. You were *perfect*."

"You set me up?" Frank was incredulous.

"Your profile also said you weren't the swiftest dog in the race. Now use your left hand to remove that gun sticking out of your pants, drop it on the road, and kick it toward me. And don't forget, I can shoot your daughter as easily as I can shoot you."

Frank dropped the gun and kicked it hard. It clattered across the pavement and was swallowed up by the wall of mist.

Wilson looked at his watch, then at Daniel. "I have no idea what this fog is, or where it's coming from—maybe a burst steam pipe. Looks like our car is out of commission. And I've dealt with that incompetent chauffeur. But if we take their pickup truck, we can still make our meeting. We'll be there in less than ten minutes, make the delivery, get the cash, and then catch our flight."

"The satellite phone?" Daniel asked.

"It's still searching for a signal. It'll let us know as soon as it's found a viable satellite and is connected. After that, it's countdown time. By then the briefcase will be in Hoboken, and we'll be on our way."

"What's he talking about, Danny? What cash? What flight?!" Conrad demanded, jumping from the back of the truck. "What have you gotten my son involved in, Wilson? Are *you* the terrorist? I entrusted you with my business, my labs, my boys' safety—my life. You're a general in the U.S. Army, for God's sake, an American soldier, a *patriot*. But I guess you're really nothing but a filthy, murderous traitor, aren't you? *My God! The bridge, the tram . . . all those people!*"

"A traitor?" Wilson laughed. "To *what?* A country with no moral values, where Presidents have sex with interns in the Oval Office, where women are promoted to be five-star generals over men like me, where gays marry each other, and where 70 percent of our citizens are too cowardly or too fat to fight for their flag?

"I've betrayed nothing—it's patriots like me who've been betrayed. But thanks to you and your money, Mr. Dinnick, I can set up my own army, establish a state where true Americans— and American values—will be embraced and defended."

"What are you talking about?!"

"Nothing you would understand, Mr. Dinnick, *sir,*" Wilson

spat out bitterly. "Frankly, you've always disgusted me. That's why I singled you out years ago to bankroll my plans. You think you're a god, but all you've ever done with your money, privilege, and power is undermine the security and the values of this once-great nation."

"I've done nothing but serve this country and save lives my entire career," Conrad said, shaking his head in disbelief.

"You've done nothing but make yourself rich off the rest of us!" Wilson yelled at him. "You convinced our so-called government that your bioscience and vaccines can defend us against terrorists. The President should have nuked all the terrorist states into submission years ago—that was our only sure method of defense. But that fool wouldn't pay attention to me because he was listening to people like you. Now they're convinced we're safe from germ warfare, when really it's only a matter of time—"

"Oh, God!" Katherine cried, her ears pounding with the sickening rhythm of marching boots, her mind reeling from the sights and sounds of soldiers . . . screaming children, street battles, tanks . . . a city in flames. "He's planning some kind of coup . . . to overthrow a government . . . somewhere . . ."

"Shut up, psychic! For someone who earns her living selling foresight, you've failed to glimpse the greatest future ever envisioned," Wilson smirked.

He turned back to Conrad. "You said I was an American soldier. Well, I *am,* but *this* is no longer my America. Thanks to your money, and your son's inventiveness, I'll soon be running my own nation-state in South America—still an *American* country, but one a man can be proud to call home."

"You're a lunatic! And you're insane to think I'd ever finance whatever evil plot you're trying to hatch!" Conrad screamed.

"You don't have to, because your son already did. Do have any idea how many mercenaries I can buy with $30 billion?"

"What $30 billion? What's he talking about, Daniel?"

"Not Daniel . . . *Michael,*" Katherine corrected, standing at Conrad's side.

"Katherine, *please,* I told you: Michael's dead and gone. Daniel is the only son I have left."

"No! *Daniel* is dead, but trust me, he's not *gone*—he's here with us now."

"Your time is up, lady," Wilson said to Katherine, leveling his gun at her. "I don't know how or why you ended up at the Tower this morning, but you've caused nothing but trouble. It's going to be a pleasure to send you to—what do you call it—the *Other Side?*"

The briefcase in Wilson's left hand beeped three times, and a thin, electronic voice announced: *Viable satellite detected. Estimated time to connection . . . five minutes.*

Wilson handed the briefcase to Daniel, keeping his gun trained on Katherine and the others. "It's almost time, son. In a few more minutes, we'll flick the switch and get out of here."

"Yes, sir," Daniel answered firmly, kneeling on the road and opening the case.

"Daniel, what are you doing—"

"Well, it's like Mr. Wilson has been saying to me for the past two years, Dad. Today is Judgment Day."

"I don't understand . . ."

Daniel looked at his father with contempt, and when he spoke, his voice was clear and even. "Dad, can you explain to me how someone who advises the President and has two Nobel Prizes can be so blind and stupid?" He laughed sarcastically.

"*Michael?*" Conrad gasped. He looked at Katherine, who nodded at him sympathetically, and then he turned back to his son.

"Michael, is it really you?"

Michael smiled. "In the flesh, back from the dead, and never to return."

CHAPTER 24

CONRAD STARED AT THE YOUNG MAN IN FRONT OF HIM in complete confusion, desperately trying to understand what was happening. "But . . . if you're Michael . . . then Danny is—"

"Dead, of course," Michael said flatly.

"Did you—"

"Kill him? No, he killed himself. I won't say I was *completely* guiltless. We had an agreement—I'd let him steal money from you, and he'd let me—"

"Danny steal from me? That's impossible. He wouldn't know how, and it would be totally against his nature."

"That's so like you, Dad. You never did give Danny any credit, did you? He was actually quite brilliant, even daring—a regular modern-day Robin Hood. You looked at him and saw a stuttering loser, but for years he was quietly siphoning billions away from you to build factories in developing countries so that they could make their own affordable medicines, instead of buying them from BioWorld. So he not only took your money, he used it to flood your biggest customer base with cheap, black-market drugs."

Conrad was stunned. What Michael was saying actually made sense. His accountants had told him only that morning that huge sums of money had "gone missing." And BioWorld's lucrative sales of antiviral drugs to the developing world had plummeted in recent years. This also explained Danny's sudden interest in working at the Hoboken lab after Michael's death— or what he'd *thought* had been Michael's death.

"You've been pretending to be Danny for two years so you could keep conducting your own experiments in Hoboken?!" Conrad asked in disbelief.

"Ah, the blind begin to see," Michael said calmly, enjoying his father's rage. "But as I was saying, I do share some of the responsibility for Danny's suicide. He knew that my experiments were illegal, and I knew about his thievery, so we agreed to turn a blind eye to each other . . . on the condition he let me use him for a few Project PAT experiments."

"My God, Michael, you didn't! PAT is years away from human trials. That's why I built the Supercomputer Re-Creation Center—to test it. Injecting Danny would have—"

"Killed him? No, I'd tested it on myself many times first, and I'm perfectly fine. But unfortunately, poor Danny developed that malignant brain tumor and couldn't face a long and painful death."

"What? No . . . if you've injected yourself with PAT, your mind must be so mixed up, your thinking so muddled. Oh, Michael, you've made yourself so sick. What have you done?" Conrad cried out.

"Don't worry about what I've done in the past. It's what I'm going to do now that will really impress you, Dad. Your Project PAT is child's play, nothing but a joke. I've gone light years beyond your research. Didn't *you* name it PAT, for *Project Aeternus Eternus*—life everlasting? But you just can't envision that, can you? All you can imagine is 'creating' transplant organs, or developing vaccines, or curing diseases. Remember when I told you that death was the sickness we had to end? That *that* should have been the goal of PAT? Well I've been working on it for years, and I'm going to do it—end cellular decay and stop the biological clock from ticking on toward death."

"Michael, son . . . only a madman would try to completely *end* the aging process. PAT was created to cure disease, to allow people to live healthier, more productive, and yes, even *longer* lives—not to conquer death. It's insane to even think it's possible—"

"No, Dad, I'm completely sane, and it *is* possible, which I'll prove in just a couple more years. All I need is my own lab, where people won't constantly question my methods. And with the help of Mr. Wilson, in a few days I'll have that lab and—"

"Wilson? How is he going to help you do anything but destroy your life? He's a paranoid, homicidal maniac."

"Maybe so, but you better remember that this 'maniac' has a gun pointed at you," Wilson broke in. He looked at Michael. "Let's cut this short, son. I can take care of them now, and we can be on our way."

"Why do you keep calling him 'son,' you psychopath?" Conrad yelled.

"Wilson's been more of a father to me than you ever were!" Michael spat out at Conrad. "And who are you to call anyone homicidal? You killed everything Danny and I ever loved. First you pushed Mother out of our lives forever, then you *murdered* Grandmother."

Conrad blanched. "What are you talking about?"

"Danny saw you kill her, saw you stick a needle in her arm and pump her full of poison until she stopped breathing. He told me everything—the image haunted him for the rest of his life, and he was never the same. Why do you think he started stuttering? He use to have such a sweet voice. Remember how he used to sing for us? But you killed that, too."

"No, no, no, Michael! No one saw that . . . you boys were in the—"

"How would you know where we were? You *never* paid attention to us!"

"I didn't murder her. She was so sick . . . in such pain. I just increased the dosage of the medication she was already on. She begged me to release her!" Conrad cried, visibly upset by the memory.

"No! You were playing God, like always," Michael said.

"No, he wasn't," Katherine countered, while placing a comforting hand on Conrad's back. She had a fleeting image of Conrad at his mother's bedside, sliding a needle out of her arm, his eyes brimming with tears as he kissed her good-bye, and his mother thanking him over and over.

"Conrad, you did what your mother needed you to do—ease her pain," Katherine said. "She thanks you for ending her suffering. I sensed that you'd caused her passing when we were in the helicopter, but I didn't see how until now. . . . She's showing me her symbol of love for you, Conrad: blue roses."

Katherine turned to Michael. "Your grandmother wants to help ease *your* pain, too, Michael. She's showing me a darkness around you . . . that you've brought a terrible sickness upon yourself . . . but I feel that the darkness isn't permanent, that you can find help . . . you must—"

"Ms. Haywood," Michael snapped in disgust, "I'm a great believer in the untapped potential of the mind. I actually believe that you possess a unique ability. You've shown consistent and extraordinary prescience throughout the day. Of course there's no afterlife, but obviously an area of your brain has developed in greater proportion to the rest of us. I'd love to have your brain removed and preserved for future study."

"I'm not quite done with it," Katherine bristled.

"You will be soon!" Wilson told her, as the computerized voice in the briefcase Michael was leaning over announced: *Satellite connection established. Trigger function operational.*

"Well, Michael, that's our cue. It's time to go. Flip the switch, I'll get the package out of the limo, and we're out of here," Wilson said.

"Just a few more minutes, Mr. Wilson?" Michael asked, suddenly looking faint and holding his head.

"What's wrong with you?" Wilson demanded.

"Nothing, I'm fine . . . I mean . . . ," Michael replied, recovering his composure. " . . . I mean, I'd like a few minutes with my dad—kind of a going-away present. He was supposed to have been killed in the helicopter, but by some incredible coincidence

I've met up with him one last time in this tunnel—"

"There are no coincidences. The fact that your production assistant found me in Italy and got me to come back here is proof of that," Katherine insisted.

"Fine, fate brought us together—whatever. It's my chance to show my dad what I'm going to achieve after he's dead. How much greater a scientist I'll be than he ever was."

"Michael, you're sick," Conrad pleaded. "All those injections have damaged your mind, and Wilson has obviously brainwashed you, but I can help. We can hire specialists—"

"Help me what? Find the real *Aeternus Eternus*—find immortality? Because that's what I'm on the threshold of finding myself, Dad. That's probably part of the reason why Danny killed himself—he realized that after all those years of arguing with me, I'd been right—God really was just a myth. It must have been too much for him to bear.

"He left a suicide note. Want to know what it said, Dad? *'Of every tree of the garden thou mayest freely eat: But of the tree of the knowledge of good and evil, thou shalt not eat of it . . .'* After all those years at divinity school, you'd think he'd come up with more poignant parting words. Let's face it, Dad, Danny just didn't have our stomach for the forbidden fruit—that lust to tease the hidden secrets from the double helix."

"That's from the Bible, what he said . . . Genesis 2:16–17!" Samantha shouted, climbing down from the cab of the pickup.

Wilson swung his gun in her direction, and Frank jumped in front of her, imploring, "Please don't. She's just a child!"

"She's a precocious little towel-head brat who refuses to die. I've memorized your profile, gardener, and the cancer should have killed her long ago."

"You're right, maybe she is a brat. She's got a photographic memory and likes to quote the Bible. She's got a big, big mouth, but she's still just a little girl."

"I'm not afraid of him, Daddy. Mom says not to be afraid."

"Shut up, Sammy!" Frank pleaded.

"No, I won't. What that other man said about tasting the

forbidden fruit, that's only part of the verse. It finishes: '. . . *for in the day that thou eatest thereof thou shalt surely die.'*"

Frank clapped his hand over Samantha's mouth.

"Shut that kid up or she shall surely die *right now*," Wilson said to Frank, then looked at Michael. "You have a green light, so flip the switch. We have to go soon or risk missing our connection."

"Mr. Wilson, please. I've done everything you've asked, and it's all in motion . . . just a few moments more," Michael said, looking at Samantha. "That's right, little girl," he told her. "If you know the Garden of Eden story, I'm sure you know that God didn't forbid Adam and Eve to eat the fruit because it would kill them, but because He was afraid it would give them the same knowledge He possessed. That it would make *them* Gods."

Samantha pushed her father's hand away from her mouth.

"No, mister, that's just what the devil said to trick Eve. In Genesis 3:4—"

"*Sammy, shut up now!*" Frank yelled.

"That's all right, let her speak. She reminds me of myself at her age. Ever have her IQ tested?" Michael asked, turning his attention away from briefcase.

"What?" Frank asked.

"Her IQ . . . did you ever have it tested?"

"What does—"

"For Christ's sake, answer the man!" Wilson yelled impatiently. "If you say *what* again, I'll shoot her."

"Yes, yes, yes, we tested her . . . it was over 200," Frank spat out. "They said it had to be a mistake. They wanted to test her again, but she got sick and I wouldn't let them."

"Over 200? Just like Conrad over there, and just like me. You know what they call that, gardener, having a 200-plus IQ?"

"Yes, some kind of genius," Frank answered, his arms wrapped protectively around Samantha.

"Some kind of genius? That's your brilliant summary? They call us immeasurable geniuses. I scored 212. Since the gene therapy, I've jumped to over 280."

"Impossible," Conrad murmured.

"Quite possible, Dad. And it's only the beginning. The potential for PAT is immeasurable." The briefcase speaker punctuated his sentence: *Trigger active: on standby.*

"What *is* that?" Frank asked, staring at the flashing lights and wires inside the case, already fearing the worst.

"That's something right up your alley, Mr. Dell," Wilson said. "It's a detonator for a dirty bomb in the basement of the BioWorld Tower. I wanted to leave this country making sure that Conrad Dinnick was not only dead, but also that the world wouldn't remember him as the great man of medical science he pretends to be. Instead, he'd be remembered as the man who spewed radiation into the heart of Manhattan."

"How did you get a dirty bomb into New York City? With all the new security precautions, it's impossible," Frank said.

"Not impossible for a U.S. Army general," Wilson snapped.

"Is that what you're using my money for, Michael?" Conrad asked incredulously. "To bomb New York and hurt thousands of innocent people?"

"What?" Michael sounded confused, and held his head in his hands again. He stared at the briefcase, then at Wilson, and finally at his father. "No . . . no . . . the Tower's been evacuated and sealed," he continued. "No one's going to get hurt . . . only the building will be contaminated. Isn't that right, Mr. Wilson?"

"Yes, that's right, son," Wilson said. "But don't start losing it now, Michael. Keep yourself together until we've made the pickup and delivery in Hoboken."

"A pickup in Hoboken? Michael, please tell me you haven't taken anything from the Level 4 lab," Conrad pleaded with him, sounding increasingly panicked.

"Well, Dad, I'd already given Mr. Wilson all the money left over from Danny's stealing so that he could hire soldiers and build my lab in South America, so we needed something else to give the terrorists in exchange for the bomb."

"Terrorists? Oh God in heaven! Michael, you didn't give

terrorists one of our viruses? You wouldn't have."

"Not one of *our* viruses, and not one of *your* viruses. It was all *my* creation," Michael said, sounding like a proud little boy.

"God, no . . . what have you made?"

"I call it Seventh Heaven, Dad."

"Seventh Heaven?"

"It's a beautiful bug; you'd be proud. A new family recipe. The engineering was tricky, but basically it's just seven extremely deadly viruses: Ebola, smallpox, Marburg, hantavirus, SARS, Lassa virus, and a dash of Spanish influenza. You mix them all together, then reduce it to an aerosol, and there you have it: Seventh Heaven."

"No, no, no," Conrad mumbled, his shoulders sagging with the realization of what his son had done. "Please, tell me you didn't."

"Oh, but I did, and it's lovely. An airborne virus that will spread like a brush fire in a high wind and has a 95 percent mortality rate. I even have the vaccine. Not enough yet, but I will as soon as . . ." Michael's voice trailed off, as though he were drifting into a stupor.

Conrad pulled himself together and shouted, "Michael, listen to me! Where have you stored it? If something like that ever gets loose . . . please, tell me it's safely stored."

"Huh? What? Of course I stored it safely, Dad," Michael responded, alert again. "It's locked up in the Hoboken Level 4, and of course, I have full access to it. In fact, we're going there now to get the new virus and give it to our friends. And then we'll leave the briefcase in the lab to make sure all your most precious buildings are destroyed. Thirty minutes after I hit this little switch, the world will remember you as it should, just like Mr. Wilson said: not as the brilliant scientist, but as the Monster of Manhattan."

"You can't do this! Son, you need help! We'll cure you, I swear. I'll move heaven and earth to help you. I'll stand by you to the end."

"Really, Dad?"

"This is the end!" Wilson broke in, slapping Michael's face. "Snap out of it, boy. I *need* you to get into the lab. Remember our plan—our mission isn't completed yet."

Wilson reached down into the briefcase, but Michael pushed his hand away. "No, it's mine . . . I'm going to do it. I'm going to play God," he whined, sounding even more like a little boy.

"Then shut up and do it!" Wilson growled.

"What have you done to my son?" Conrad demanded.

"Nothing. Nothing at all. Whatever he is now, it's because *you* made him that way," Wilson snapped. Then he yelled at Michael again: "Do it now!"

At the sound of the harsh command, Michael suddenly came out of his daze. He put his finger on the gold switch.

"Wait, mister," Samantha said. "You don't want to destroy everything, do you?"

Michael paused, looking at Samantha. "I'm not destroying, kid, I'm creating. How would you like to play a little game my brother and I used to play when we were kids? We called it 'Creation.' I said everything started with the big bang. He said everything started with God. Do you know anything about creation myths?"

"Yeah, lots—and my name is Samantha, not kid," Samantha said.

"All right, *Samantha*, the Egyptians believed that—"

"Nun, the God of watery chaos created the—"

"Very good," Michael said, running his finger over the switch. "How about the Africans?"

"Which ones?"

"Oh, let's say . . . Zulu."

"The creator Unkulunkulu brought people to the earth," Samantha answered.

"Hey, gardener, your kid's a real brainiac—too bad she's dying. I'll need bright people like her when I set up my new world," Wilson told Frank. "She must have gotten her smarts from her towel-head mother, because you're clearly a moron."

"My mother says you're a bad, bad man!" the little girl announced.

"Really? You talk to her?" Wilson asked with a gleam in his eye. "Well, say hi for me. Last time I saw her was when I gave the order to have her shot so I could set up your daddy. Don't worry, though, I made sure she died quickly."

"You goddamn murdering bastard—you killed Sarah!" Frank screamed, rushing at Wilson.

Wilson cocked the hammer of his gun and pointed it at Samantha's head.

"Frank, stop! The child!" Conrad yelled.

Frank stopped dead, eyes wild with rage, his chest heaving.

"You may not be very bright, Dell, but you *are* an arms expert. Tell me . . . what am I holding in my hand?" Wilson asked.

"A .44 Magnum," Frank rasped through clenched teeth.

"Is it an effective weapon?"

"Extremely."

"Then if you don't want me to use it on your kid, I suggest you step back against the truck and don't move again. Let Samantha and Michael finish their nice little chat so I can get him out of here before he loses his wits completely."

"This isn't a nice chat," Samantha said to Wilson. "And my mom says that you're sicker than I am . . . and that she's looking forward to seeing you real soon."

"Isn't that sweet," Wilson smirked.

The circle of fog that had been surrounding them began closing in, becoming denser and brighter.

Michael looked into Samantha's dark eyes. "You've got guts, kid, I'll give you that. Now come on, let's finish our game . . . what about Buddhism?"

Samantha crossed her arms in front of her chest. "I'm not playing anymore," she said.

"Samantha, please, *for me?* Answer him!" Frank pleaded.

"Okay . . . for you, Frank. Buddha began his journey toward enlightenment after leaving his palace as a little prince and wandering among the poor and sick and—"

"Right on the money. How about the Hindus?"

"Hindus believe that the thousand-headed God of Immortality, Purusha, wrapped his arms—"

"You've almost won the big prize," Michael praised.

"Mister, it doesn't matter what different people in different places believe about how the world began. Almost all of them believe that our spirit moves from this world to the next. That it's how we live our life, not how life began, that's important, and that—"

"Now you're sounding like my brother," Michael said wearily. He shook his head. "I just have one last question, Samantha. What about the Jews and Christians?"

She answered, "Out of the void and chaos God said, 'Let there be light.'"

"Right again," Michael answered. "Now, here's your prize. Something you've never read or heard anywhere—not a creation myth, but a creation *fact*. It goes like this: *And in the tunnel deep beneath the waves, Michael Dinnick wrapped his finger around the switch and said 'Let the New World begin.'*"

He began to push the switch but stopped. He stood up, looking around, lost and bewildered. He looked at his father, and then he looked at Wilson.

"I can't," he said. "People . . . people . . . will be *hurt* . . . Mr. Wilson . . . please don't make me."

"You sniveling wimp!" Wilson yelled, shoving him out of the way as he bent down, stuck his hand in the briefcase, and flipped the switch. Then he turned and faced the group, pointing the gun at Conrad. "You go first, Dinnick."

But before he had a chance to pull the trigger, a single beam of light pierced the mist, followed by the high whining of a fully revved, rapidly approaching engine.

Wilson shielded his eyes against the blinding brightness of the motorcycle's high beam. He pointed the gun toward the light and pulled the trigger.

The shot echoed down the tunnel.

The intense blue light of a .38-caliber muzzle flash pierced the thick mist.

Wilson's hands flew up to his chest, pawing briefly at the gaping wound that tore through his heart, before he collapsed onto the road.

The Harley burst through the wall of mist. Jack was holding his service revolver in one hand, trying to control the bike's handlebars with the other. Zoe clung to Jack as he hit the brakes, sending the motorcycle into a tire-screeching skid. The big bike dropped onto its side and came sliding toward them in a shower of red and orange sparks.

"Daddy!" Samantha shouted.

Frank grabbed his daughter and jumped into the rear of the truck.

The motorcycle's front tire hit Michael just below the knees, tossing him high in the air.

He vanished into the fog.

CHAPTER 25

"SAMMY, ARE YOU ALL RIGHT?"

"You're crushing me, Frank."

"Sorry."

Frank sat up quickly and noticed that the fog was thickening around them. He lifted his daughter and held her tightly against him—she felt cold again, and her pulse was weak. He wanted to run out of the tunnel with her, but he still couldn't see anything beyond the mist engulfing them.

Samantha began choking, gasping for breath. Noticing that her pale skin was turning blue, Frank ripped off a strip of material from his shirttail and wrapped it around her mouth.

"Breathe through this, sweetie. Maybe it will help."

He peered into the darkness. There was nothing, just the harsh sound of her labored breathing.

"Is anyone else alive?" he shouted. His voice sounded muffled, lifeless in the fog.

"I'm okay, I'm right behind you. I'm not hurt," Katherine said.

"Try to get into the back of the truck. God only knows what will happen if another vehicle comes through here," Frank said. "Conrad, are you out there? Are you okay?"

They could hear him somewhere in the distance, calling out for his son.

"Michael, where are you?"

There was no reply.

"Conrad, come back to the truck! Don't get lost in the mist—there's something very strange happening here!" Katherine called out.

Conrad's voice grew fainter. "Michael . . . where are you, son? Michael . . . come to me, come to your father."

"Conrad, get back here!" Frank yelled. "Jesus, I can't see more than a foot in front of my face. We need some light."

Samantha began to cough harder, a deep rattle echoing in her chest.

Frank heard someone crying several yards away and called, "Who's out there?"

The crying stopped. A gentle female voice was softly pleading for someone to get up. Then the gentleness faded, and the voice grew increasingly stern and demanding: "You stop this, Jack! Do you hear me? You said you'd get me through this. Now say something to me right now! Wake up! Wake up, you crazy bastard!"

They heard the sound of flesh slapping flesh.

"Ouch! Jesus Christ, I've been shot. You didn't have to hit me, too, didja?"

"Oh, Jack, thank God you're alive," Zoe squealed. "You're shot? Where? I don't feel blood."

"I've been shot enough times to know when I've taken a bullet and—ouch, ouch, ouch."

"I found where you were hit."

"I noticed—hey! Watch your hands, woman!"

"Relax. I need to get your belt off so I can use it as a tourniquet. You've been hit in the right thigh, and there's a lot of blood. But you're lucky; I think the bullet missed the femoral artery. "

"Suddenly you're a doctor."

"Basic Red Cross field training, and I used to hang out at the morgue a lot."

"The morgue? I don't want to hear about it . . . but how can you tell the bullet missed my—whaddaya call it? My immoral artery?"

"*Femoral* artery. I know it's not severed because if it was, you'd have bled to death by now. But it could be nicked, so shut up while I tighten this belt." Zoe continued to work on him.

"Forget about me. How are *you?*"

"I'm fine. I did like you said and just held on to you. The only thing that hit the ground was my backpack and head. If I hadn't had your helmet . . . but what was that Wild West show you put on before we crashed? Who are you, Quick Draw McGraw? You're not getting crazy on me again, are you?"

"I dunno . . . I saw a guy with a gun, and something or someone guided my hand. Believe it or not, after all those years of being a cop, that was the only time I ever fired my service revolver."

"Well, whatever it was, you only had that one bullet—the one with your name on it. So I take it you won't be shooting *yourself* anytime soon?"

"Let's take it one bullet at a time," Jack grimaced, as Zoe tugged on the belt.

Frank had been listening to the conversation without a clear sense of where the voices were coming from. He felt like he was lost at sea, unable to gain his bearings.

"Where are you—*who* are you people?" Frank asked again.

"My name is Zoe Crane," she answered. "I'm a reporter, and I have a wounded police officer with me. His name is Jack Morgan."

"Does the headlight on your bike work? We need some light," Frank asked.

"Not a chance, pal. It's more busted up than I am," Jack said wryly. In a softer tone, he asked Zoe, "Do you have matches?"

"No, but I have a flashlight in my bag. Just a second . . . oh damn! It's smashed. Oh, wait, there's a spotlight on my palmtop!" Zoe yelled.

A faint orange dot appeared near Frank.

"That's your spotlight?" he asked incredulously.

"No, that's the Record-Active light. The camera's recording, but the spotlight is broken . . . and the damn cigarette smokers in my office must have stolen my matches and lighter."

"So we've got to find our way out of here in the dark?"

Zoe snapped her fingers. "Maybe not. I just remembered that I've got something else in my bag that might work."

There was a crack, then a small pool of red light opened up the darkness.

Emergency road flare, Frank realized, looking down at Samantha. He placed his hand on her chest, distressed by its feeble rise and fall. Pulling the cotton cloth from his daughter's face, he peered into her eyes as best he could in the dim light. Her pupils were glassy and unfocused.

"Oh, my sweet girl, hold on," he whispered.

She drew a crackly breath that made his heart pound. The whistling in her lungs was identical to the noise made by a wounded soldier he'd once carried to a field hospital. The man—only a boy, really—had two punctured lungs and labored for breath as Samantha did now. That soldier had died in Frank's arms.

"We're almost home now, right, Daddy?"

"Almost, Sammy. Just hold on a little while longer."

It was difficult for Frank to catch his own breath. He felt light-headed and struggled to assess the situation rationally. *We'll all die in here like rats. Oh, Sarah, please help me.*

"Don't be frightened," Samantha whispered. "Mommy hears you."

Her voice was so faint that Frank couldn't make out what she was saying. "Don't speak, Sammy, save your breath," he told her, then turned in the direction of the road flare that was illuminating Zoe and Jack.

"Hey, lady—I mean, Zoe, do you have any more flares with you?" Frank asked.

"No, just that one, and it's old. It might last 20 minutes, tops," Zoe answered.

"Why are you carrying a flare, anyway?"

"Because I'm a reporter, and I covered 9/11 from Ground Zero with nothing but a notebook and pen. After that, I vowed never to go anywhere in this city without my emergency bag."

"What else have you got in there?"

"What do you need? Water, bandages, disinfectant, a thermal blanket, a radiation meter, anti-radiation pills, a stun gun, superglue, a tube of Chanel lipstick, two tampons, an oxygen canister, a whistle—"

"Oxygen?"

"Yeah, one canister—30 minutes' worth."

"Please, my daughter can't breathe—"

"One second," Zoe said, tightening Jack's belt just below his hip. "You stay put," she told him, carrying her bag to the pickup and getting her first look at Samantha.

"Oh, she looks really sick—," Zoe started saying, handing Frank the small oxygen cylinder.

"I've got to get her out of here, but this fog . . . I can't move anywhere, and I can't figure out what it is or where it's coming from," he said, putting the oxygen mask over Samantha's mouth.

Frank began twisting the tiny airflow knob at the end of the cylinder. "Damn it, it's stuck! Which way does it turn?" he asked nervously. "I don't want to snap it off . . . I need more light!"

"Wait," Zoe motioned, pulling her camera from the bag. "The damn digital video recorder won't shut off, so everything is being taped, but the LCD screen should be a little brighter."

She held the palmtop's small, glowing screen over the canister, giving Frank enough light to see the arrow pointing left. He twisted the knob, and the cylinder hissed softly.

Samantha's breathing eased immediately. Her eyes focused on Frank's, and she smiled at him.

"Mom says, 'Hello,' Daddy, and . . . she heard you."

"Yeah? Tell her 'Hey' right back. But for now, I need you to lie still and breathe slow and deep," Frank told his daughter, easing her down on the tailgate. He picked up two rolls of sod, tossed them toward the flare, and turned to Katherine.

"Please watch her for just a second. I'm going to try to make her more comfortable until this steam, or whatever it is, passes."

"Of course," Katherine replied.

"I'm going to make you a little Kentucky bluegrass bed, okay, Sammy? I'll be back in a flash."

"Peachy-keen, jelly bean." Samantha smiled.

Katherine squatted down beside her and took her hand.

"Sarah's with you, isn't she, honey?" Katherine whispered.

The little girl nodded and smiled. Then she pointed at Zoe's computer.

"What's that?" Katherine asked Zoe as she glanced at her palmtop.

"A palmtop computer. They're new—it's a computer, phone, video camera—"

"No," said Katherine. "I mean, what's the picture on the screen?"

Zoe looked down. "That's the last image in the still-photo memory. I took it just before I left the office this morning. I forgot all about this! It's a picture of the mannequin the police found under the Queensboro Bridge before the explosion. Maybe that was where the bomb was planted."

"Can you enlarge it?" Katherine asked.

"I paid $18,000 for this thing; I better be able be to enlarge it," Zoe said, pressing a button. The image painted on the mannequin's torso came sharply into focus.

Katherine gasped. "The Tower card! That's the reason I'm here."

CHAPTER 26

"IT'S A TAROT CARD!" ZOE BLURTED OUT, remembering the lesson her assistant had given her on the ancient tools that some psychics used in their work.

"Not just any tarot card, but one of the most powerful of the Major Arcana," Katherine explained.

"Why do you think someone would paint it on the mannequin?"

"I have no idea, but if this was the bomb that brought down the bridge and destroyed the computer center, maybe it was a last laugh at Conrad—the man who built the world's largest tower."

The two women stared at the frightening image filling the computer screen—a bolt of lightning striking a gray, lighthouse-type tower, shattering its top and setting it on fire. A king's crown toppled toward the ground as people plummeted through the air toward the earth.

"God, it looks like what happened at the World Trade Center," murmured Zoe.

"Well, that's often what the card represents: sudden and unexpected change—which is often destructive and irreversible."

"Just like what's happening now."

"It would seem that way," Katherine agreed. "But the Tower card can also mean positive change when things seem like they're at their worst, like the arrival of a new child, or the beginning of a happier phase in one's life. It's a burst of universal energy, a force that affects a major turning point in a person's path. A friend once told me that I'd have to help interpret this card at a crossroad in my life—and I think I'm at that point right now."

"I think we all are," Zoe replied.

Katherine stared at Zoe in sudden recognition. "You're that reporter who earns her living writing nasty things about psychics—including me—aren't you?" she asked.

"Well, it hasn't been much of a living," Zoe replied.

"Maybe that's about to change . . . we'll have to wait and see," Katherine said.

Frank returned to the truck. "How's my girl?" he asked.

Zoe gave him the thumbs-up. He lifted Samantha out of the truck, making sure her oxygen mask didn't slip off.

"Let's gather 'round that flare and figure out what to do to get out of here," Frank said.

"Good idea," agreed Zoe, placing her palmtop on the hood of the pickup, its small orange Record light flashing like a tiny beacon in the mist.

They all moved toward the red glow of the road flare, where Jack was sitting propped up against the wreckage of his Harley. Frank laid Samantha down carefully on the mattress of soft grass he'd prepared for her. Zoe squatted beside Jack to check his leg— even though no main arteries or veins had been severed, it was a nasty wound and still bleeding heavily. She dug into her bag for her first-aid kit and brought out some thick cotton bandages and a roll of gauze.

"Jeez Louise, it looks like a shark chomped on you," she muttered, placing the dressings over the wound and winding the gauze around it a dozen times. "Jack, put your hand on the bandage and keep pressure on it, okay? Now, you're still losing a lot of blood, so I'm going to tighten the belt around the wound, and it's going to hurt like hell."

Zoe looked him in the eye, and Jack smiled at her. She

pulled the belt as tight as she could, and he kept smiling.

"You have an incredibly high threshold for pain."

"You have no idea," he said, reaching out and brushing Zoe's hair from her eyes. "Are all the nurses in this tunnel as pretty as you?"

"Jack Morgan, you *are* crazy. Earlier this morning you were planning to blow your head off, and now you're flirting with a complete stranger."

"I'm not flirting, and once you've been on the back of my Harley, you're no stranger."

In the dim light, she could barely make out his face. She touched his hand and whispered, "Jack, I'm really scared."

"Don't worry. I told you I wouldn't let anything happen to you. See how well I'm protecting you? You're trapped 100 feet underwater with a crippled old cop, breathing in a vapor made of only God-knows-what—"

"Stop it! I told you: You're not *old.*"

She sat beside him. The group had formed a little circle around the flare like kids sitting around a campfire.

They sat in silence, shrouded in the persistent fog and at a complete loss as to what to do or say about the surreal situation in which they were trapped. For those few moments, the only sound in the tunnel was the steady hiss of Samantha's small oxygen tank. Then they heard Conrad, emerging from the mist, calling out for help. His son was slung over his right shoulder, and Wilson's briefcase was in his right hand.

"He's badly hurt. Please help me lay him down," Conrad pleaded, moving into the small circle of light. Frank jumped up and helped get Michael to the ground.

"Is he alive?"

"Yes, but it doesn't look good. He was barely conscious when I found him . . . and Wilson's dead," Conrad paused, then collected himself and pointed to the briefcase. "And that is a very, *very* serious problem," Conrad noted, laying the case on the road and opening it up.

An electronic voice startled them: *T-minus 25 minutes.*

"If what Michael said is true, then in less than half an hour this thing is going to set off a radioactive bomb in my Tower—*in the middle of Manhattan!*" Conrad's voice rose. He sounded increasingly panicked.

Frank knelt down and studied the briefcase. Twenty-six wires, each marked with a different letter of the alphabet, ran from the satellite phone into a block of plastic explosives as thick as a phone book and twice as wide. The neon numbers on the digital clock attached to the top of the plastic flashed rhythmically, counting down to zero.

"It's an ETD," Frank said.

"What's that mean?" asked Conrad, his voice now thin and weak.

"An explosive triggering device. When the timer runs down, the phone signals a receiver to detonate whatever it's wired to, and then this transmitter will self-destruct. That means this briefcase will blow up. And there's enough explosive in here to knock a hole the size of a house through this tunnel and let the entire Hudson River come pouring in on us."

"Can you turn it off?" Conrad asked, kneeling beside Frank.

"No."

"Please . . . you have to . . ." He grabbed Frank's arm tightly.

"I wish I could, but I can't. I'm taking my daughter to New Jersey, to a hospital. And far away from you and Manhattan and this mess you've made possible—"

"No, Frank, please! I'm being told you have to disable it now!" Katherine said firmly, putting her hand on his shoulder. "There's powerful energy all around me. I feel the presence of a female figure, a wife . . . it's a love bond. And she has an 'S' name . . . like Susan, yes, Susan. But your wife's name is Sarah—I'm confused. There are two 'S' names, two wife energies coming through together. . . ."

Frank brushed her hand away. "And exactly who's telling you all this?"

"*They* are—the spirits."

"Listen, Katherine," Frank spat out angrily, "there are 26

wires here! If I cut the wrong one, this thing will detonate, and then we'll all be dead. So if your supposed spirits can tell me which wires to cut, how many to cut, and in what sequence to cut them, I'll do it. Otherwise, Sammy and I are outta here."

The briefcase squawked: *T-minus 21 minutes.*

"No! You have to listen. They insist! *You can do this.* You can defuse this before it's too late. Sarah says—"

"Don't say my wife's name to me again! She's dead. I don't believe in what you do, and I don't have any time to waste. That oxygen tank is all that's keeping my little girl alive, and the air is running out!" Frank yelled, hot tears flooding his eyes as he looked at Samantha lying on the patch of bluegrass.

"Do you know what will happen if you leave without at least *trying* to stop this thing?" Katherine pleaded.

"Yes, I do, and I also know what will happen if I stay," Frank answered, watching Samantha cough into her mask, small pink bubbles forming at the corners of her mouth.

For the second time since they'd entered the tunnel, he closed his eyes and silently asked for help he didn't believe existed.

Please, Sarah, show me what to do!

CHAPTER 27

THE ROAD FLARE SPUTTERED AND DIED, leaving them in complete darkness except for the eerie, unnatural glow of the mist swirling around them. The hiss of Samantha's oxygen tank stopped abruptly.

Then the tunnel was suddenly alive with voices. The fog thickened, and a dazzling burst of blinding light flooded the group. Rays of a thousand different colors shimmered about them as if they were in the center of a crystal prism.

A heavy layer of mist rolled over them, so impenetrable that Frank lost sight of everyone, even Samantha, who'd been lying right beside him.

Then he heard her voice, at least a dozen feet away. He jumped up and ran toward the sound as the fog moved around him like a river, filled with shifting pools and eddies. For a moment, the air cleared, and he saw Samantha skipping in circles near the edge of the deepest bank of fog.

"Daddy, Daddy . . . we're inside a rainbow," she giggled, before she was once again shrouded in mist. He heard her voice clearly but could only catch glimpses of her as she moved through the cloud.

"Sammy, stay put for a minute. Let me look at you," he laughed. "You look so . . . so . . . healthy! Are you feeling better?" he asked in wonderment, stretching his arms out to her for a hug.

"You're silly. Of course I feel better," she continued skipping. "I told you: We're *here*."

"I know we're here, honey; we're still stuck in the tunnel. But I can hear voices and see lights, so there must be a rescue party nearby. Now come over here and give me that hug."

"Frank?" Katherine said carefully.

"Not now," Frank replied with some impatience, delighting in the sight of his daughter skipping happily.

"Daddy, you won't forget, will you?"

"Forget what, sweetie?"

"About my bench in Central Park."

"I promise, Sammy, but you won't need that bench, not for a long, long time. Come here, now."

"Frank . . . ," Katherine persisted.

Samantha performed a little pirouette and a curtsy.

"Thank you, kind sir," she said, giggling again.

"Frank, *please!*" Katherine pressed a third time.

"Listen to Katherine, Daddy. She's talking to Mommy. I'm not going anywhere yet."

"She's 'talking to Mommy'?" Frank asked. He looked at Katherine, who was gazing at Samantha in amazement. The psychic's face was glowing, a serene smile lighting her face as tears rolled down her cheeks.

"What's wrong? Why are you crying?" Frank asked, confused.

"It's so beautiful, more beautiful than I ever imagined," she whispered. "I can hear them all so clearly . . . it's like the most wonderful music. . . ."

"Who can you hear?"

"It's who you thought, Frank. It's a rescue team, but it's not going to be the kind of rescue you were expecting," Katherine explained softly.

"What do you mean? Sammy, where are you? Where'd you go?"

Frank was suddenly alone with Katherine, but vaguely aware of the others still there, standing in the luminous pool of light.

"Listen, Frank—*all of you,* listen to me," Katherine said gently. "There's a veil between this world and the next, a very thin veil. Few people realize that energies on the Other Side are continually trying to communicate with us. We either block them out because we're too afraid to listen, or because we just refuse to believe they exist. But right now, here in this tunnel, something unbelievably special is happening that I've never experienced before—*something wonderful.* The veil is being lifted."

She turned to Frank, taking both of his hands in hers. "Frank, your daughter has a wonderful gift she's been trying to share with you for a very long time, but you've never allowed yourself to open your mind—to open your heart—and accept her offer. She's been a patient teacher, but you've been a poor student. You've allowed your pain and grief to build a wall between you and the love you never really lost, the love of your family . . . Sarah's love."

"What are you telling me?"

"I'm telling you that your eyes have been open, but you've failed to see what Sarah's been trying to show you: that she's there for Sammy, ready to help her cross over to the Other Side and begin her new journey. The same way Sarah's mother, Fatima, was there to greet her when she passed over."

Frank looked at Katherine, beginning to panic.

There was no way she could have known that Sarah's mother's name was Fatima . . . unless she really could talk to the dead. He was terrified—not only of the enormity of what he was hearing, but by all the years he'd refused to believe Samantha when she insisted Sarah was still with them.

"You're ready, Frank. Turn around," Katherine said softly.

Frank turned, but he couldn't understand what he was seeing. "No," he whispered, and closed his eyes. *It's not real, it's not real, it's just a dream.* He opened his eyes, and then he did something he hadn't done for years. He crossed himself.

Standing before him was his wife, her beautiful face framed by soft, dark curls . . . her eyes looking at him with such love.

"Sarah," he moaned. "Oh, I'm sorry, I'm so sorry . . . so sorry," Frank said, falling to his knees.

"Sarah, my sweet love, where have you been? Why did you leave? Please come back . . . come home to me. I miss you, I *miss* you . . . I've tried to be a good father to Sammy, to raise her the way you would've wanted, but it's been so hard without you . . . she's been so sick since you left, and she needs her mother back . . . oh, please, Sarah." Frank's throat was swollen with the words and feelings he'd buried so deep, that had burned unspoken in him for so long.

Sarah smiled at him but said nothing.

"She hears you, Frank, and I hear her . . . more clearly than I've ever heard anyone from the Other Side. She says you've been a wonderful father, and she knows how much you love her. She carried your love with her when she passed and feels it still. She says your love fills her . . . but she also says you threw something away because of her, and it pains her. She says you must embrace it again, Frank. You must find what's been lost."

"I don't understand." Frank shook his head in confusion.

Sarah's image began to shimmer, slowly retreating into the mist.

"Wait . . . oh God, not again, don't leave me again!"

"She has to go, Frank. What do you want to tell her?"

"That I'm sorry. I'm sorry that I was angry at you when you left . . . oh, Sarah, please forgive me for not kissing you good-bye. . . ."

Sarah's translucent face was suddenly only a breath away from Frank's. He looked into her eyes and felt the fire of her lips brush softly across his, then she was gone . . . and Frank slipped to the ground, his hands covering his face as he laughed and cried and cried and laughed.

"Daddy?"

Frank looked up. Through his tears, he watched Samantha blow him a kiss.

Oh, Sammy, I was going to dance at your wedding, he thought.

Samantha winked at him and said, "Don't worry, Daddy, me

and Mommy will dance at *your* wedding."

Then Sarah took Samantha's hand in hers—and together his daughter and his wife smiled at him . . . and walked away into the mist.

THE OTHERS HAD BEEN WATCHING in stunned silence.

Katherine spun around and looked at Jack. "Do you hear that, Captain?"

Jack heard the clanging bell of a fire truck sounding deep within the tunnel. Not a real fire truck, but a toy, like the one he'd given Liam on Christmas morning many years ago. He could see nothing in the white fog until Katherine stepped in front of him.

"There are two strong energies coming through for you. One's the female companion figure who came through earlier today." Katherine smiled. "Now I understand why two female 'S' energies were coming through to me: first Sarah for Frank, and now *Susan* for you.

"She's laughing at you . . . she says your back wouldn't hurt so much if you'd stop sleeping on the sofa bed in the guest room."

"Susan . . . Susan . . ." Jack repeated softly, watching in disbelief as she slowly materialized before him. She was wearing her wedding dress and holding out her left hand, pointing at the tiny diamond he'd placed on her ring finger when they took their vows.

"She says, 'The smallest diamond shines the brightest.' She's laughing again—what a kind, funny energy she has, Jack. And tender . . . so tender. She's worried about you, though. She says your life is yours to live—not to throw away."

"I see her, I see so clearly," said Jack. "But I can't hear her voice."

"She hears you, Jack, and she's repeating what she said this morning: 'Forgive yourself . . . stop dying and start living' . . . now she's laughing again."

Then, for the first time since they'd climbed into that

carriage in Central Park the night she was killed, Jack heard the music of Susan's soothing, loving voice.

"I can hear her . . . I can hear her lovely, sweet laughter . . . I can hear my beautiful wife!"

"She wants to know who you've been fooling around with on the Harley. . . . She says she's cute," Katherine laughed. "Susan says to help the pretty girl find what's been taken from her, and you'll find what *you* need. Her energy is pulling back."

Jack reached up to stroke Susan's face as she began to fade into the air. He touched her, and his entire body flooded with warmth. For the first time in years, he felt no physical pain at all.

"Don't go!" he begged, reaching out into the fog to touch Susan one last time. Instead, he found Zoe's hand waiting there for him, so he took it in his and squeezed tightly.

Then Susan was there again, holding a little boy by the hand. She vanished, leaving the boy with Jack.

"Liam! It's my son! I see him, but . . . he's just a boy. Liam!" Jack stared at the little fellow, who was wearing his favorite pair of cowboy pajamas and holding the new toy fire engine in front of a Christmas tree.

"You're seeing him the way you love remembering him most," explained Katherine. "But I'm also seeing a uniform, flames . . . a plane crash. He passed violently, but very, very quickly. It was an honorable passing. He was, oh, dear Lord, when he died, he was in—"

"The World Trade Center. He was one of the first firefighters in the building. We never found him," Jack wept, his chest heaving as he squeezed Zoe's hand.

The image of small Liam morphed into a handsome young man in a firefighter's uniform.

"He's showing me that day. He carried a lot of people out of the tower. He kept going back in . . . he was a hero, Jack. He wants you to know he felt no pain—and no regret. He passed doing what he wanted to do, saving lives. But he says he feels *your* pain—he says it's all around him. He wants me to tell you that suicide is never the answer. That you only end up hurting others and yourself."

"But I feel like I *did* hurt him. The last time we spoke, I was angry at him. I never even said good-bye."

"Are you carrying something of his? He's showing me a badge, or some kind of medal."

Jack reached in his pocket and pulled out the medal he'd received after Liam's death. He wanted to show it to Liam, but when he looked up, his son was gone.

"He sees it, Jack. And he says to tell you to remember what that badge means, to honor his memory and his sacrifice, not to let the pain of his passing destroy you. He's repeating Susan's words: *Forgive, live, love.*"

Jack couldn't see Liam, but he heard his son's voice as clearly as though the boy were standing beside him.

"I know how much you loved me, Dad, and how proud you are . . . but you've been locking yourself inside your house, and outside of your heart. That changes today. This is my ultimate rescue. Let me rescue *you*, Dad."

Liam reappeared for a moment, smiled at Jack, then looked at Zoe and said, "You'll be a great mom."

Liam's image began to fade. "Remember . . . it all changes today, Dad."

"Zoe, there's a female energy here for you," Katherine told her. "It's a mother energy, but not a birth mother. You were adopted," Katherine said with realization.

"Me? . . . Yes, I was," Zoe said, feeling intensely uncomfortable.

"This energy, it's so heavy . . . I can barely stand under the weight of her remorse . . . her name is Abby . . . or—"

Zoe saw a shadow hovering behind Katherine. "Her name is Abigail, and she can go to hell, if she isn't there already!" she screamed.

"She understands your anger, Zoe. She's showing me a crown, like a tiara. That usually means victory and achievement to me . . . but this tiara is black . . . pain and suffering and loss . . . it's attached to so much loss. Do you understand any of this?"

"You bet I do," Zoe said bitterly.

"She wasn't a very nice person . . . not a good mother to you," Katherine continued.

"She was evil."

"She wants your forgiveness, Zoe. She knows how badly she hurt you, that she wounded your heart and made it so difficult for you to trust . . . to love."

"It's typical of her—she wants my forgiveness, but she won't even show her face to ask for it herself."

"She wants to show herself to you, Zoe, but even here, in this tunnel of light, your emotions are so dark that they're blocking her out," Katherine said.

"Tell her to leave me alone! I'm not interested in what she has to say!" Zoe sobbed, squeezing Jack's hand, which had never left hers.

"She's showing me a hospital . . . a maternity ward. . . . Did she force you to give up a child?"

"Please stop, Katherine! I don't want to remember."

"She doesn't expect you to forgive her, Zoe, even though she wants it very much. She accepts responsibility for what she did, but she wants to help you. She says a pony came to you recently . . . or something by pony express. Does that make sense to you?"

"A pony? Yes, a picture of a pony on a letter. It came in the mail today, and I pinned it up over my desk at the office . . . but why would she—"

"Do you have a daughter?"

"No, I don't . . . I mean, I don't know, I'm not sure . . . they wouldn't let me see—," Zoe began weeping. "I had a baby! I had a baby, and they took it away from me. I don't know if I had a boy or a girl. All I know is I had a baby, and I've never held it in my arms."

"She says to find the girl who sent the letter, the pony girl, and you'll find your daughter . . . that's Abigail's way of show-ing you her love, Zoe."

The dark shadow behind Katherine flared briefly to a vibrant pink before it withdrew into the mist.

A dog barked in the distance. "Rewrite? That's Rewrite! That's my puppy," Zoe said in amazement.

"That's one more way Abigail is trying to reach you with love. She wants you to know that Rewrite is okay . . . and wait-ing for you."

KATHERINE LOOKED AT FRANK, JACK, AND ZOE. She felt a sense of peace among them, but could sense a wave of pain behind her. She was being pulled toward Conrad and Michael—she knew she was needed.

Conrad was staring into the wavering haze and strange vapor that had isolated him from the rest of the group. Kather-ine's voice was coming at him from all directions, and high above him, he heard a child's playful laughter.

Conrad held Michael's head in his lap, caressing the bruised and battered face of a man, but remembering him as a boy, espe-cially the trusting eyes with which his son had always looked upon him.

I pressured you too hard to succeed. I pushed you too far, right over the edge of sanity, Conrad thought. *And Danny, poor Danny, I drove him away—all I cared about was my work, and all I achieved was killing everything I ever loved.*

He looked up. Katherine was beside him, smiling. "Your *sons* are here; both of them are with you now. One on this side, one on the Other Side. And there's the mother energy that's been around you all day . . . that's always around you. . . ."

"No, this can't be. There must be a gas leak . . . I must be hallucinating. This can't be happening," Conrad murmured. But then he looked up, and his heart began to melt.

"Mother?"

He saw her through the fog, sitting at her workbench in the greenhouse back in Iowa. Her hair was pinned up, the way it always was when she worked; and she glowed with the vibrant, lush beauty of youth and health.

The scene was cloudy, like the kind you'd see in the swirling liquid of a just-shaken snow globe. But as the vision became clearer, he recognized the exact moment in time: It was his 8th birthday . . . she was just 30, and so lovely . . . then he was beside her. She was showing him a flower . . . he could hear her words echoing back to him from the past. . . .

It's your turn to try, Connie. If a farmer's wife can play God, I don't see why a farmer's son can't, do you?

His heart was pounding . . . it was her birthday present to him, his first glimpse into the wonders of DNA, into the secrets of life itself. The vision clouded, diminishing . . .

"She has great regret, Conrad. She says she was wrong to tell you to play God," Katherine said. "She wishes she'd told you to *embrace* God, in whatever way, in whatever form you could . . . that all you ever needed to know exists within that embrace."

Michael stirred in Conrad's lap and sat up, looking at Katherine in bewilderment.

"She's pulling back . . . she's sending love to you, showing me blue roses . . . again, she's thanking you for easing her pain, for helping her pass. She's gone, but she's bringing through a male energy . . . a very old soul. His energy has also been with us all day."

"Where? I can't see anything," Conrad said.

"He says he's sorry for leaving the way he did, for the pain he caused by taking his life. He says not to remember the way he passed . . . but remember the song."

"Is it Danny? What song? What song does he—"

Suddenly, Conrad was sitting in a school auditorium more than 30 years ago, with a young Michael by his side. It was a special night, a rare occasion where he'd taken time from work to attend one of his boys' school events. Danny stood in the center of the stage, his face beaming with pride as spoke to the crowd.

I dedicate this song to Conrad Dinnick, my dad, and to my best friend in the whole world—my brother, Mike, Daniel said clearly, with no a trace of a stutter.

"Michael, look, it's Danny . . . look there . . . Danny's back!" Conrad exclaimed.

Michael's eyes widened. He whispered: "It's Danny's song."

Danny began to sing in a sweet, lyrical voice that seized Conrad's heart.

> *Oh Danny boy, the pipes, the pipes are calling*
> *From glen to glen, and down the mountain side*
> *The summer's gone, and all the flowers are dying*
> *'tis you, 'tis you must go and I must bide.*
> *But come ye back when summer's in the meadow . . .*

"Danny, please forgive me," Michael muttered, getting to his knees. Conrad sobbed, as the light on the stage brightened so intensely that Danny appeared translucent.

> *And if you come, when all the flowers are dying*
> *And I am dead, as dead I well may be*
> *You'll come and find the place where I am lying*
> *And kneel and say an "Ave" there for me.*
> *And I shall hear, tho' soft you tread above me*
> *And all my dreams will warm and sweeter be*
> *If you'll not fail to tell me that you love me*
> *I simply sleep in peace until you come to me.*

The stage light waned. Danny, now a grown man, stood before his father and brother, his arms across his chest, hands clasped above his heart.

"He says he's at peace, but asks your forgiveness—and he wants both of you to forgive yourselves, and each other," Katherine said.

"Danny!" Conrad and Michael cried out in unison.

"He's showing me *he's* healed, but he needs you to know that you can heal each other—it's not too late. You *can* find the cure in the embrace. He's pulling away . . . he's gone. . . ." Katherine's voice trailed off.

KATHERINE DROPPED TO THE TUNNEL'S FLOOR, alone in the mist, utterly drained.

Never in her life had she felt the energy of spirits surge through her with such force and power. It was as though she'd stepped across to the Other Side and, for a few brief, glorious moments, had walked among them, talking to them effortlessly, hearing them with complete clarity. She actually felt their thoughts and emotions as they had them.

She realized that the Other Side had needed her here to be a conduit to the people she'd been thrown together with today. Her presence had been necessary, but this had drawn on every ounce of her psychic ability. She knew it was an honor—but it was an honor she never wanted to have again.

Since the energies had retreated, she was left with only silence . . . and a sense of overwhelming loneliness. She was more exhausted than she'd been in Italy, more tired than she'd ever been in her life.

She barely had enough energy to keep her eyes open.

I'm crossing over, she thought. *I'm spent . . . I'm finished.*

CHAPTER 28

"HI, KATHY. THERE'S SOMEONE HERE WHO WANTS TO TALK TO YOU."

Katherine opened her eyes and saw Samantha's smiling face looking down at her. There was an intense but lovely expression in the child's eyes. Her skin glowed with a rosy hue in the shifting light.

"Sammy, am I—," Katherine began to ask.

"Of course not. Don't be silly," Samantha scoffed.

"Are you—"

"So many questions from someone with a visitor waiting to see her," she giggled.

"What visitor?"

"Her," Samantha said, pointing behind Katherine, but the exhausted woman continued to stare at the girl's gleaming smile. Then she felt a presence behind her emanating such intense love that she was afraid to turn around. She closed her eyes as the familiar strains of Sinatra filled her mind.

> *. . . painted kites, those days and nights went flying by . . .*
> *. . . then softer than a piper man, one day it called to you . . .*
> *. . . and I lost you—to the summer wind . . .*

"Don't be afraid, Kathy," Samantha said gently.

Katherine opened her eyes and saw the friend she'd loved more than any other, the person who'd believed in her and opened her mind to a world of books and music and wonderment. The person who'd guided her to her life's work, and whose absence had left a gnawing emptiness.

"Julia," she whispered, "where have you been? Why have you never come through to me? Why did you leave me all alone?"

"She says you should know why," Samantha said. "You knew each other so well that you'd never believe it was her if she *did* come to you. You'd think you were tricking yourself into believing."

Samantha's laugh echoed in the mist. "She says you must be losing your touch—she's been sending you messages since Italy to get here. . . ."

"The tower images?"

"You got it!" Samantha exclaimed.

"Julia, I need you. I'm so, so weary . . . I can't go on with the work. I have nothing left to give anyone."

"She's asking me who you are," Samantha relayed.

"She can't see me? She doesn't know?" Katherine cried in confusion, tears streaming down her cheeks.

"Oh, she sees you, all right. But she says the Katherine Haywood she knew wasn't a quitter—she's strong, a warrior."

"I have no fight left . . . I can't help anyone anymore."

"She says to stop it. You've helped *everyone.* You've turned the Tower card around, you've drawn the light from the darkness, turned negative force into positive energy . . . and now she says to reach out."

"Reach out where?"

"To *her,* silly. She says to put out your hand."

Katherine offered her hand to her old friend and felt an electrical current run up her arm and around her skull. A flash of white light exploded in her mind, and she could feel Julia's presence in every cell of her body as strength and energy pulsed through her.

For a moment she saw her father and grandmother standing beside Julia.

"I told you that you were special, sweetheart," her father said, beaming. "You just had to grow into your specialness."

"Remember to look both ways before crossing the road, little Kathy," her grandmother chuckled sweetly.

"Oh, Dad, Grams . . . I love you," Katherine whispered, as her family faded from view. She stretched her arms wide and breathed deeply, feeling renewed and regenerated.

"My God, I've never felt so . . . alive," she said in wonderment.

"Her gift to you," Samantha explained, smiling, "but she still has something to say to everyone here."

Julia's image became brighter than any they had seen so far, and suddenly they could all hear her voice: "You've been given a gift, each of you. You've looked into a world few ever see without first being touched by death. You were brought together to heal yourselves, to know you can move forward, and to understand that you must use the time allotted to you on this physical plane to grow, to learn, and to love. These lessons you must share with others beyond the walls of this tunnel—especially the lessons of love and forgiveness—because that's what endures and binds all our energies together."

"But—," Zoe began to say, unsure of how to address this vision.

"Your question is about *him*," Julia said, looking through the clearing mist at Wilson's lifeless body, barely visible a few yards away.

"Yes," Zoe said. "How can we love or forgive someone like him . . . is he in hell? Or does evil energy exist where you are?"

"His hell is to realize, relive, and personally experience the same pain he's inflicted on others. He must atone for his actions . . . and has much to atone for . . . but he will."

Katherine looked up at Julia as the image began to waver and fade.

"Julia! Will I hear from you again?!" Katherine cried out.

"We're always together, Katherine, and we'll be together again, but not yet. Your work is far from over. Remember what I told you the first day we met. Even the darkest tunnel can open up onto the brightest of lights, and right now there are many dark tunnels in the world. New York is just the beginning; your mission is destined to take you to many places. You have a light, Kathy, and you must let it shine," Julia said, and she was gone.

A fog enveloped the group, leaving everyone but Katherine in a semiconscious state.

Katherine looked to Samantha to thank her for bringing Julia through. The girl was gone, but she could hear her voice.

"Please, Kathy, help my daddy."

Somewhere in the tunnel, an electronic voice announced: *T-minus five minutes.*

"WAKE UP, WAKE UP! Wake up now, Frank!" Katherine shouted, shaking him violently by the shoulders.

"What's the matter, Sarah?" Frank asked sleepily. "It's Saturday morning, my turn to sleep in—*your* turn to take Sammy to temple. . . ."

"It's not Sarah, Frank; it's Katherine. Get up—the bomb is about to go off!"

"What . . . what's happening?" Frank said in confusion, sitting up and looking around groggily. "Sammy . . . where's Sammy?"

"She's safe, Frank . . . but the rest of us aren't."

"What?!" he exclaimed, now fully alert.

"Frank . . . the bomb!" Katherine screamed.

T-minus two minutes.

"Oh my God! Two minutes? Jesus, it's too late for any of us to get out!" Frank realized, crawling over to the briefcase and peering inside at the many wires and flashing lights. "I can't . . . I can't—"

"Yes, you can, Frank. Sarah is telling me you must find what you threw away when she died."

"I don't know what you mean! I have no idea! The bomb

. . . its trigger is too complicated. I gotta think . . . I gotta think."

"You think too much, Frank. Listen to your heart," Katherine told him. "Find what you lost when Sarah died."

Frank thought of Sarah's funeral. He remembered standing by the coffin, dropping his crucifix inside before he closed the lid, the crucifix his mother had given him before his first communion, engraved with the words: *Franco, Non perda mai la vostra fede.* Frank, never lose your faith.

He reached into his jeans, pulled out his pocket knife, and held it over the mass of wires.

T-minus 1 minute.

Frank opened the blade and put it under the wire with the letter *F* stamped on it. He hesitated. Then he thought he heard Samantha's voice behind him.

"It's in your heart, Daddy."

T-minus 30 seconds.

He took a deep breath and sliced through the *F* wire. Nothing happened.

He moved the knife expertly, like a surgeon, and cut through the *A* wire, then the *I*, the *T*, and the *H*.

There was a hard metallic click, and the speaker in the briefcase announced: *Countdown aborted at T-minus 9 seconds.*

The fog began to lift.

"I don't understand what's happening," Frank said, looking behind him through the thinning mist to the small patch of grass where he'd left Samantha. There, he saw her lifeless body, with the plastic oxygen mask still strapped across her face.

The howl formed in the center of his being, churning in his gut until the pain forced it into his throat like a fist, breaking through his mouth and screaming down the length of the tunnel like a wounded animal.

A single, heart-wrenching "Noooooooooooooooooooo!"

"Shhhhhhh, Frank, it's all right." Katherine tried to comfort him as she knelt beside him.

"Oh God, Sammy, don't leave, don't leave me here alone

. . . don't go—"

"She's already gone, Frank, but you know she hasn't left you," Katherine told him with conviction, placing her hand over his heart. "She says she'll always be right here . . . just never lose faith."

Frank collapsed onto the asphalt.

EPILOGUE

THE STATIC FROM THE RADIO IN THE PICKUP TRUCK WOKE HIM UP.

Frank rolled onto his side and saw that the truck had returned to life, its headlights cutting a double path of light leading to the end of the tunnel and illuminating the bodies scattered on the road. The radio emitted a low, crackling buzz.

As he walked toward the patch of green, he could hear everyone breathing and saw that they were all beginning to move—all but Samantha.

Frank kneeled beside her and carefully removed her oxygen mask, wiping the traces of blood from her lips and chin.

"Sammy," was all he could say, leaning down to kiss her forehead and cross her arms over her chest.

Her right hand was balled into a fist. He gently opened her fingers and saw it glitter in her palm: the cross he'd dropped into Sarah's coffin.

It can't be . . . it just can't be . . . but here it is!

With tears in his eyes, Frank took the crucifix from her hand and kissed it. Then he slipped the gold chain around his neck, and tucked the cross into his shirt.

He felt Katherine's hand on his back. "The world is full of miracles, Frank—big and small. We just have to look for them. She's all right, you know. She's happy, she's safe, and she's with Sarah."

"I know she is," he admitted tearfully, getting to his feet and looking at the psychic.

"But . . . are *you* okay, Frank?"

Tears streamed down his face. "No, I'm not . . . but I know I will be. She taught me how to live, and how to believe. But it's so hard. It's so difficult to know *what* to believe."

Katherine put her arms around him, hugging him tightly while he sobbed on her shoulder.

"It takes time, but it will come to you," Katherine said compassionately.

Behind them Zoe was leaning over to help Jack get up, but he bounced to his feet before she had the chance.

"Hey, be careful, Jack, your leg! You'll hurt yourself getting up so quickly. Are you okay?" she asked.

"I've never felt better in my life," he told her. He glanced at his leg—his wound was healed. Then he looked into Zoe's soft green eyes, took her hands in his, and kissed both.

"Wow," she said, with a surprised smile.

"Thank you," he told her as he gazed at her appreciatively.

"For what?"

"For everything you've done for me, starting with the stun gun—when you shocked me back into the world of the living."

"Well, you're welcome, and thank *you!*"

"For what?"

"For everything you're *going* to do for me. . . . because I know you're going to help me find my baby . . . my daughter."

Conrad had lifted Michael to his feet and was walking with him toward the others. Michael seemed dazed.

"What happened, Dad? Where are we?"

"You got sick, Michael . . . and you've had an accident. But we're going to get you better, I promise. I know just what to do. You're going to be fine—we're both going to be fine."

Conrad and Michael stood beside Frank and Katherine.

Conrad looked down at Samantha. "Oh, no! Frank, I'm so

sorry. Oh, God . . . I know how painful it is to lose a child . . . and to almost lose another. I—I don't know what to say." Conrad hugged him.

Zoe ran over to Frank and threw her arms around him. "She was a beautiful, beautiful girl!" she exclaimed.

"She *is* a beautiful girl. She *is*," Frank said.

"I've been where you are, and I know there isn't much I can say to ease your pain, except that she's part of all of us now, and always will be," Jack told him.

Frank acknowledged Jack with a nod, and then they all stood in silence, looking down at Samantha, each saying farewell in their own way.

Then they looked at each other, no one quite sure what to say or where to start.

"Do we all know what we've just been through?" Katherine asked.

Everyone nodded.

"But no one outside this tunnel is ever going to believe it," Jack said.

They were all silent again.

"Then let's not tell anyone else. What happened in the tunnel stays right here," Frank suggested.

"Except that I've got this," said Zoe, picking up her palmtop from the hood of the truck. "I've been writing about this stuff for so long, but I never believed a word of what I wrote . . . and now that I finally have proof, I don't need it."

She popped the disk out of her small computer. "It was recording the entire time. Everything that happened is probably documented on this—it's the story of a lifetime."

They all looked at her, waiting, expectant.

Zoe took a deep breath and sighed. "Oh, well. My horoscope this morning said to perform a selfless act, and that it was time for a career change." She laughed, handing the disk to Katherine. "It's yours to do with what you want."

Katherine smiled, putting the disk into her pocket. "Welcome to your crossroads," she said to Zoe.

"Look, everyone, this is far from over!" Conrad said. "Just for starters, there's a new virus in my Hoboken lab I have to take care of—and no one outside this tunnel should ever know about it. Agreed?"

"Agreed," they all said.

"There's also a dirty bomb in my Tower in Manhattan that we have to try to defuse quietly so we don't panic an entire city."

"I should be able to handle that," Frank volunteered, "but something that serious is going to be hard to keep quiet."

"I have friends in high places who can help keep a lid on it. It's not something they're going to want to advertise," Conrad said, looking over at Wilson's body on the road. "As far as my son is concerned, he'll have to answer for whatever part he played in what happened at the bridge and for any other crime he's committed. And finally, there's a group of terrorists in Hoboken waiting for Wilson to show up with a package."

Conrad turned to Jack and said, "I never had a chance to thank you for saving my life. So thank you. Are you really a cop?"

Jack checked his watch. "I'm on the payroll until five o'clock. But I'll get the information about the terrorists and Wilson to the right people: the police, the FBI—whoever it takes."

"Okay, but before we do anything, we have to get out of this tunnel," Frank said. "Neither of these vehicles are going anywhere, so it looks like we're walking."

Conrad went first, his arms around Michael to support him as they left.

Zoe turned to Jack. "Do you need a hand to walk?"

"Do I look like an old man to you? I'll race you to Joisey."

"No, just walk beside me, Jack," Zoe told him, taking his hand.

Frank bent down and lifted Samantha into his arms.

"Do you want some company, or should I leave you alone?" Katherine asked.

"No, please walk with us," Frank said, as he began the final journey with his daughter to the end of the tunnel. "She really liked you, Katherine—you understood her so well. I wish I could have done that sooner."

"Oh, no, Frank, don't regret anything. All I could see was how close she was to the Other Side. You had her love, and you knew her heart."

"It's going to be hard without her . . . not hearing her voice."

"You know, Frank, you *will* be hearing from Sammy again."

"I know I will," Frank said, then smiled. "Sammy would laugh if she heard me quoting the Bible, but there's something she used to say to me all the time that just popped into my head: *There are three things that last forever: faith, hope, and love. But the greatest of them all is love.*"

THE HIGH BEAMS ON THE TRUCK cast them all in silhouette against the growing light at the end of the tunnel.

The static on the radio was slowly replaced by the sharp, clear voice of a female reporter:

"*. . . is improving as the solar storm moves away from Earth's atmosphere and into deep space. The electrical grid is slowly getting up and running again, and telecommunication systems around the world seem to be coming back online.*

"*Here at Action News, our field reporters are starting to call in with some amazing stories. As I've said already, this has been a phenomenal day in New York City. The main explosion on Roosevelt Island that severely damaged the Queensboro Bridge has been extinguished, and city engineers say initial estimates are that the bridge could be completely repaired within six to eight months.*

"*The mayor and governor and many City Council members are being treated for abrasions and broken bones after the Roosevelt Island Tram they were riding in dropped safely onto a sand barge passing beneath the bridge moments before it collapsed.*

"*Once again, as remarkable as it sounds, everyone who was on the bridge at the time of the explosion seems to have escaped with minor injuries, and while the numbers are not yet final, at this moment we have no confirmed reports of any fatalities—no fatalities at all.*

"It's seldom you'll hear a news anchor say this, but folks, if I was told I had to sum up today's events in one word, that word would have to be: miraculous!"

ACKNOWLEDGMENTS

Sandra—your unconditional love and support allows me to do everything that I do.

Justin—you're the reason I can't wait to come home . . . always remember that Daddy loves you.

Carol—if I could get you to stop stealing pens from hotels and my desk . . . some might consider you perfect. . . .

Isobel, Lucille, John, Ruth, Phil, and Kelly—a special thank you and all my appreciation for always going above and beyond in all that you do.

Joanne—you will always be King of the Forest to me.

Jolie and Roxie—you're still my girls.

Jon—wooooooooooooooooooooooooooooooooooooooooosh!

Stacy—thank you for your continued support and friendship and . . . you know!

Reid Tracy—thank you . . . again and again and again.

Jill Kramer, for all that you do.

Gina Rugolo—your enthusiasm and energy are such a help in my achieving my professional goals.

Marc Chamlin—thank you for your sage advice and counsel and for always being there.

Corinda Carford—you are my sage.

Jill Fritzo—for your hard work, support, and friendship.

Natasha Stoynoff—a few years ago you were brought into my life to write a story about the subject matter of life after death. That turned into a great friendship that took us across the world, where you helped me write Part III of my journey in this work. Now . . . I think we've found a great place where both our creative minds have come together to tell a story that will be entertaining, and enlightening as well. I look forward to what's next. . . .

Steve Erwin—(no, not the crocodile guy!), thanks for all your invaluable help you gave to your wife, Natasha, on her spiritual adventure.

There are so many other people that I could mention here, but that would be another book all unto itself. I know you all know who you are. . . .

— **John**

———————————

Thank you to my beautiful colleagues at *People* magazine, who hid me when I slipped in late and wrecked after all-night writing sessions.

Many thanks to Lou Stanek, for her much-needed guidance.

Many thanks to Jill Kramer, who didn't complain when I begged for deadline extensions and then worked miracles.

Much gratitude to sweet Miss Mellie, aka Norris Mailer, for her constant encouragement and inspiration. Put Paris and our Southern epic on the to-do list. . . .

Thank you to the loved ones on the Other Side whom Steve and I miss terribly, and who helped write this book. You know who you are. Come and visit more often.

Thank you to John Edward, a fellow number "9," who had the movie version of this book cast even before we'd written the first word! Thanks for your invaluable friendship, patience, trust, and Other Side insight. You have enriched my life.

And most of all, thank you to my dear husband, Steve, whose endless talent, ideas, research, energy, faith, passion, and too many years of watching bad-brother movies all added up to help make the finest moments in this story.

— **Natasha**

If you enjoyed *FINAL BEGINNINGS* and want to continue
with this spiritual adventure to see what happens next,
look for *INFINITE ENDINGS* . . . coming soon . . .

ABOUT THE AUTHORS

John Edward is an internationally acclaimed psychic medium, and author of the *New York Times* bestsellers *One Last Time, Crossing Over, After Life*, and *What If God Were the Sun?*. In addition to hosting his own syndicated television show, *Crossing Over with John Edward*, John has been a frequent guest on *Larry King Live* and many other talk shows, and was featured in the HBO documentary *Life After Life*. He publishes his own newsletter and also conducts workshops and seminars around the country. John lives in New York with his family.

For more information, see John's Website at:
www.johnedward.net

Natasha Stoynoff is a staff correspondent for *People* magazine, and this is her fourth book collaboration, following *Life's Little Emergencies* with supermodel Emme; *Never Say Never* with former CBS sportscaster Phyllis George; and *After Life* with John Edward. She has worked as a news reporter/photographer for *The Toronto Star* and as a columnist for *The Toronto Sun*. Her work has also appeared in cover stories for *Time* magazine. Natasha lives in Manhattan with her husband, writer/journalist Stephen Erwin, and is currently working on her first screenplay.

THE JOHN EDWARD NEWSLETTER
"BRIDGES"

The John Edward newsletter, "Bridges," is a quarterly magazine-style publication that includes:

- Inspirational stories
- A Q & A "Ask John" section
- Spiritually related areas
- Reader validations and experiences
- Special subscriber offers
- Guest contributors
- Other related material

To order your subscription of the "Bridges" newsletter, just fill out the order form. In addition, as a special gift from John for purchasing **both** this book and a *"Bridges"* newsletter subscription, you will receive three (3) *free* John Edward Appreciation Pins (a $20.70 value).

Due to overwhelming demand, you must send the original form below, not a copy.

Please make check payable *(in U.S. dollars only)* to **Get Psych'd, Inc.**, and mail your order to:

Get Psych'd, Inc.
P.O. Box 383
Huntington, NY 11743

Allow 4–6 weeks for delivery.

Visit our official Website at: **www.johnedward.net**

Name_____

Street Address_____

City_____State_____Zip_____

Phone_____E-mail address_____

Check appropriate box:

❑ **1-year subscription: $24.95***   ❑ **2-year subscription: $39.00***
*Please include $2.95 for shipping and handling. Thank you.

*Plus 3 **Free** John Edward Appreciation Pins*

We hope you enjoyed this Princess Books publication. If you would like more information about Princess Books, you may contact the company through their distributor, Hay House, Inc.:

Hay House, Inc.
P.O. Box 5100
Carlsbad, CA 92018-5100

(760) 431-7695 or **(800) 654-5126**
(760) 431-6948 (fax) or **(800) 650-5115 (fax)**
www.hayhouse.com

Distributed in Australia by:
Hay House Australia Pty. Ltd., • 18/36 Ralph St. • Alexandria NSW 2015 • *Phone:* 612-9669-4299 • *Fax:* 612-9669-4144 • *E-mail:* info@hayhouse.com.au

Distributed in the United Kingdom by:
Hay House UK, Ltd. • Unit 62, Canalot Studios • 222 Kensal Rd., London W10 5BN • *Phone:* 44-20-8962-1230 • *Fax:* 44-20-8962-1239 • www.hayhouse.co.uk

Distributed in the Republic of South Africa by:
Hay House SA (Pty), Ltd., P.O. Box 990, Witkoppen 2068 • *Phone/Fax:* 2711-7012233 • orders@psdprom.co.za

Distributed in Canada by:
Raincoast • 9050 Shaughnessy St., Vancouver, B.C. V6P 6E5 • *Phone:* (604) 323-7100 • *Fax:* (604) 323-2600